INTRODUCING
ISSUES WITH
OPPOSING
VIEWPOINTS®

Self-Driving Cars

Lisa Idzikowski, Book Editor
Pete Schauer, Book Editor

GREENHAVEN
PUBLISHING

Published in 2019 by Greenhaven Publishing, LLC
353 3rd Avenue, Suite 255, New York, NY 10010

First Edition

Articles in Greenhaven Publishing anthologies are often edited for length to meet page requirements. In addition, original titles of these works are changed to clearly present the main thesis and to explicitly indicate the author's opinion. Every effort is made to ensure that Greenhaven Publishing accurately reflects the original intent of the authors. Every effort has been made to trace the owners of the copyrighted material.

Library of Congress Cataloging-in-Publication Data

Names: Idzikowski, Lisa, editor. | Schauer, Pete, editor
Title: Self-driving cars / edited by Lisa Idzikowski and Pete Schauer.
Description: First edition. | New York : Greenhaven Publishing, 2019. |
  Series: Introducing issues with opposing viewpoints | Includes
  bibliographical references and index. | Audience: Grades 7–12.
Identifiers: LCCN 2018005847| ISBN 9781534503632 (library bound) | ISBN
  9781534503649 (pbk.)
Subjects: LCSH: Autonomous vehicles—Juvenile literature. | Transportation,
  Automotive—Safety measures—Juvenile literature. | Automobiles—Automatic
  control—Social aspects—Juvenile literature.
Classification: LCC TL152.8 .S44 2019 | DDC 388.3/42—dc23
LC record available at https://lccn.loc.gov/2018005847

Manufactured in the United States of America

Website: http://greenhavenpublishing.com

Contents

Chapter 3: Will Self-Driving Cars Become the Norm in the Next Ten Years?

Foreword

Indulging in a wide spectrum of ideas, beliefs, and perspectives is a critical cornerstone of democracy. After all, it is often debates over differences of opinion, such as whether to legalize abortion, how to treat prisoners, or when to enact the death penalty, that shape our society and drive it forward. Such diversity of thought is frequently regarded as the hallmark of a healthy and civilized culture. As the Reverend Clifford Schutjer of the First Congregational Church in Mansfield, Ohio, declared in a 2001 sermon, "Surrounding oneself with only like-minded people, restricting what we listen to or read only to what we find agreeable is irresponsible. Refusing to entertain doubts once we make up our minds is a subtle but deadly form of arrogance." With this advice in mind, Introducing Issues with Opposing Viewpoints books aim to open readers' minds to the critically divergent views that make up our world's most important debates.

Introducing Issues with Opposing Viewpoints simplifies for students the enormous and often overwhelming mass of material now available via print and electronic media. Collected in every volume is an array of opinions that captures the essence of a particular controversy or topic. Introducing Issues with Opposing Viewpoints books embody the spirit of nineteenth-century journalist Charles A. Dana's axiom: "Fight for your opinions, but do not believe that they contain the whole truth, or the only truth." Absorbing such contrasting opinions teaches students to analyze the strength of an argument and compare it to its opposition. From this process readers can inform and strengthen their own opinions or be exposed to new information that will change their minds. Introducing Issues with Opposing Viewpoints is a mosaic of different voices. The authors are statespersons, pundits, academics, journalists, corporations, and ordinary people who have felt compelled to share their experiences and ideas in a public forum. Their words have been collected from newspapers, journals, books, speeches, interviews, and the internet, the fastest-growing body of opinionated material in the world.

Introducing Issues with Opposing Viewpoints shares many of the well-known features of its critically acclaimed parent series, Opposing

Viewpoints. The articles allow readers to absorb and compare divergent perspectives. Active reading questions preface each viewpoint, requiring the student to approach the material thoughtfully and carefully. Photographs, charts, and graphs supplement each article. A thorough introduction provides readers with crucial background on an issue. An annotated bibliography points the reader toward articles, books, and websites that contain additional information on the topic. An appendix of organizations to contact contains a wide variety of charities, nonprofit organizations, political groups, and private enterprises that each hold a position on the issue at hand. Finally, a comprehensive index allows readers to locate content quickly and efficiently.

Introducing Issues with Opposing Viewpoints is also significantly different from Opposing Viewpoints. As the series title implies, its presentation will help introduce students to the concept of opposing viewpoints and teach them to use this material to aid in critical writing and debate. The series' four-color, accessible format makes the books attractive and inviting to readers of all levels. In addition, each viewpoint has been carefully edited to maximize readers' understanding of the content. Short but thorough viewpoints capture the essence of an argument. A substantial, thought-provoking essay question placed at the end of each viewpoint asks students to further investigate the issues raised in the viewpoint, compare and contrast two authors' arguments, or consider how one might go about forming an opinion on the topic at hand. Each viewpoint contains sidebars that include at-a-glance information and handy statistics. A Facts About section located in the back of the book further supplies students with relevant facts and figures.

Following in the tradition of the Opposing Viewpoints series, Greenhaven Publishing continues to provide readers with invaluable exposure to the controversial issues that shape our world. As John Stuart Mill once wrote: "The only way in which a human being can make some approach to knowing the whole of a subject is by hearing what can be said about it by persons of every variety of opinion and studying all modes in which it can be looked at by every character of mind. No wise man ever acquired his wisdom in any mode but this." It is to this principle that Introducing Issues with Opposing Viewpoints books are dedicated.

Introduction

"Many say that America has a love affair with the automobile. It is a symbol of personal freedom—the ability to go wherever you want, whenever you want. It has provided point-to-point transportation … for more than a century. And …as we all know, transportation is on the verge of the most significant transformation since the introduction of the automobile. Automated or self-driving vehicles are about to change the way we travel and connect with one another. This technology has tremendous potential to enhance safety … Automated vehicles hold the promise of not only improving safety, but increasing access to mobility … for our elderly and people with disabilities (and) could provide millions with security, freedom and a better quality of life."

—US Secretary of Transportation
Elaine L. Chao, January 14, 2018

The future and what lies ahead has always meant different things to various generations of people. Before the invention of the printing press, books and other printed materials were nonexistent or very rare. This scarcity ended with the invention of the press, and consequently, learning and literacy became possible for many individuals. Much later in history, scientists engineered for decades and manufactured a reliable combustion engine that could be used to provide methods of transportation. Every day, people hardly think twice about jumping into their car and rushing to school or work or taking off in a plane to any number of far-flung destinations. And what about life-saving penicillin? After accidental discovery, this antibiotic drug was eventually mass-produced, and even today it saves many lives by curing once deadly infections.

President Abraham Lincoln once said that "the best way to predict your future is to create it." But if it were possible to see down the long road of the future, would that highway be crowded with driverless cars? In 2014, the Pew Research Center conducted a survey of American adults and asked their opinion about what scientific technology may bring about in the next fifty years. Were self-driving or autonomous cars on the minds of these respondents? Amazingly, 48 percent said they would be interested in riding in a driverless car, while 50 percent said they would not. Another 39 percent believed that teleportation would be possible by then, and 33 percent were convinced that humans would be living on extraterrestrial planets. Interestingly, the respondents also wished for three futuristic inventions: flying cars and bikes or personal aircraft, the ability of time travel, and improvements in health care that extend human life spans and cure major diseases.

The concept of driverless cars has been around for quite some time. By the 1950s experimentation with early stage automation had already occurred, and by 1987 a self-driving prototype was introduced by Carnegie Mellon University. Proponents of autonomous cars point to positive outcomes, often increased safety, better mobility for certain individuals, an overall reduction in traffic deaths, a cleaner environment, and less congested cities. They reason that texting drivers, aggressive drivers, and tired or confused drivers would no longer be in the equation, replaced by the cameras, computers, radar, and laser systems used by autonomous cars.

This argument sounds reasonable, but the American public doesn't see it that way. In fact, their trust in autonomous technology is not increasing or remaining stable; it is falling. Studies conducted by the Massachusetts Institute of Technology (MIT) in 2016 and 2017 revealed a distinct decrease in preference for or trust in self-driving cars, across all age ranges. The largest drop occurred in the 25- to 34-year-old age range, with 40 percent willing to use a fully autonomous car in 2016, but only 20 percent willing to use a self-driving car in 2017. In the same survey, another question asked whether an individual would consider purchasing a driverless car. A whopping 48 percent answered that "I would never purchase a car that completely drives itself." Various answers were given for the decision, but loss of control, mistrust in the vehicle, its safety, and reliability were the most common reasons cited. Those in fear of the technology might be comforted by Marie Curie, who once said, "Nothing in life is to be feared, it is only to be understood."

For the moment, the American public can rest easy. At a recent Consumer Electronics Show, the annual trade convention where the best and biggest of new gadgets and gizmos make an appearance, auto executives and others connected with the future driverless car technology contend that it will be years before a truly autonomous car arrives on the market and that major hurdles in its development are still ahead. The technology of robotics and artificial intelligence is changing rapidly, but perhaps not as rapidly as we might think. For instance, Toyota's demonstration vehicle may appear at the 2020 Tokyo Olympics but will likely not be completely ready to launch. At Hyundai, 2021 is the year the company expects to be testing a level 4 self-driving vehicle on city routes. At Lyft, the company expects to be hiring human drivers for a very long time, and in fact predicts that number to grow in the next ten years to keep up with demand of service. True level 5 autonomy is coming, but according to a researcher at Toyota, that date is in the future and unknown. The current debate about the technology of self-driving cars is explored in the viewpoints of *Introducing Issues with Opposing Viewpoints: Self-Driving Cars*, shedding light on this interesting and important contemporary issue.

Chapter 1

Are Self-Driving Cars Safe?

Autonomous vehicles are an exciting possibility.

Autonomous Vehicles Can Reduce the Number of Teen Traffic Accidents

Allison Crow

"If all US teen drivers traded car keys for the Waymo service, we could eliminate one million accidents and countless teen fatalities."

In the following viewpoint, Allison Crow analyzes whether self-driving cars are safe. Using Waymo, formerly called Google's Self Driving Car program, as the basis for her argument, Crow cites that Waymo has driven more than 2 million miles within the United States and was found to be at fault in only one accident, which equates to an at-fault rate forty times lower than that of new (teen) drivers. Crow goes on to write that if all US teen drivers used the Waymo service, it would result in 1 million fewer accidents and consequently fewer fatal accidents on US roads. Crow is a chemical engineer specializing in energy efficiency in the transportation industry and is an associate working in the Rocky Mountain Institute's (RMI) Mobility practice.

"How Safe Are Self-Driving Cars?," by Allison Crow, May 1, 2017. ©2017 Rocky Mountain Institute. Published with permission. Originally posted on RMI Outlet. https://www.rmi.org/news/safe-self-driving-cars/.

AS YOU READ, CONSIDER THE FOLLOWING QUESTIONS:
1. According to this viewpoint, how many deaths per year in the United States are caused by drivers aged sixteen to twenty?
2. As stated by Crow, what is delaying the development of autonomous vehicles?
3. What advantages do autonomous vehicles display, according to Crow?

On Tuesday, Waymo (formerly called Google's Self Driving Car program) announced a bold new step in the deployment of electric automated mobility services that will eventually reduce CO_2 emissions by almost a gigaton per year and help limit global temperature rise to less than 2 degrees. Hundreds of Arizonans will be accepted into a pilot program to use Waymo autonomous vehicles to go about their daily business (within a radius around several areas near Phoenix—no Vegas road trips yet).

Waymo has logged over two million miles on US streets and has only had fault in one accident, making its cars by far the lowest at-fault rate of any driver class on the road—about 10 times lower than our safest demographic of human drivers (60–69 year-olds) and 40 times lower than new drivers, not to mention the obvious benefits gained from eliminating drunk drivers.

However, Waymo's vehicles have a knack for getting hit by human drivers. When we look at total accidents (at fault and not), the Waymo accident rate is higher than the accident rate of most experienced drivers. Most of these accidents are fender-benders caused by humans, with no fatalities or serious injuries. The leading theory is that Waymo's vehicles adhere to the letter of traffic law, leading them to brake for things they are legally supposed to brake for (e.g., pedestrians approaching crosswalks). Since human drivers are not used to this lawful behavior, it leads to a higher rate of rear-end collisions (where the human driver is at-fault).

The High Cost of Teenage Drivers

Motor vehicle accidents are the leading cause of death of teenagers in the United States—with as many as 8,000 deaths per year caused by drivers ages 16–20. Released to the roads by themselves after only a few months of training, the overwhelming new freedom and responsibility leads to immature and dangerous decisions. In addition to causing the largest percentage of vehicle fatalities, AAA found teen drivers cost the American society over $34 billion annually. This includes medical expenses, lost work, property damage, quality-of-life loss, and other related costs.

If every teenage driver in Phoenix took Waymo instead, there would be as many as 12,000 fewer accidents per year. If all US teen drivers traded car keys for the Waymo service, we could eliminate one million accidents and countless teen fatalities. Since we allow teens to drive on our streets, it makes sense that we should allow autonomous vehicles—a safer option—to drive on our streets as well.

We Can't Let Fear Guide Autonomous Vehicle Policy

Many cities, states, and federal agencies are actively encouraging autonomous vehicle deployment, but this is not universal. Some politicians are trying to delay autonomous vehicles out of genuine fear of the technology and others from fear of disrupting major business such as auto dealers and insurance companies. Additionally, the new technology has not yet gained the same level of trust as other transportation systems, further holding back deployment.

A 2017 study by Deloitte found that three-quarters of Americans do not trust autonomous vehicles. Perhaps this is unsurprising as trust in new technology takes time. Comparably, air flight took many years before most people lost fear of being rocketed through the stratosphere at 500 mph in a pressurized tube propelled by exploding jet fuel. But few air travelers bat an eyelash now, calmly completing crossword puzzles and productively working on wifi as if it's normal for humans to fly.

The trust in technology takes time. However, with five automobile fatalities occurring every hour, we do not have time for fear to delay autonomous vehicle deployment. While autonomous vehicles

New drivers, which are usually teen drivers, account for a sizable percentage of traffic accidents. Can self-driving cars reduce incidents of teen accidents and fatalities?

may still be in their equivalent of Drivers Ed, we must embrace this phase of autonomous vehicle deployment in order to reap the potential benefits of tens of thousands of saved lives and millions of avoided accidents.

Autonomous Vehicle Pilot Projects

A near-term solution is for autonomous vehicles to prove themselves in demonstrations and pilots not unlike the way teenagers drive first with parents and instructors. To this end, RMI is developing autonomous vehicle pilots and programs on the ground in Austin, as a means to promote their commercial deployment and legality, and drive adoption by consumers. Determining the bar for driverless vehicle legality is critical. It must be fair when compared to our bar for human drivers. Once an autonomous vehicle and software meet this bar, it should graduate to a full license and be allowed full access to the roads. This is how society has taught every driver to drive, why not keep the same process for computer drivers?

Fortunately, this awkward phase will not be long, as autonomous vehicles learn much faster than their teenage human counterparts. Unlike a 16-year-old driver, autonomous vehicles know what to do in countless road scenarios, never forget their lessons, and never get drunk or text. In the long run, whom would you rather encounter on the road—a newly licensed teenage driver or an autonomous vehicle? And down the road, what if every driver you encounter is the best driver in the world? An interesting thought for your next road trip.

EVALUATING THE AUTHOR'S ARGUMENTS:

In this viewpoint, Allison Crow analyzes whether autonomous vehicles are safe. She primarily focuses on self-driving vehicles for teenagers, comparing data from auto accidents that occur with people ages 16 to 20 in the United States. Based on what you read, do you believe that self-driving cars would be a safer option for teen drivers?

Tesla's Autopilot Feature Isn't Fully Safe Just Yet

"The company said this was the first known death in over 130 million miles of Autopilot operation."

Joan Lowy and Tom Krisher

In the following viewpoint, Joan Lowy and Tom Krisher write about an accident that took place in a Tesla car in which the Autopilot feature was used. This incident marked the first fatality in the United States in which self-driving technology was employed. Lowy and Krisher argue that, far from being fully autonomous, the Autopilot feature still requires that the driver keep both hands on the wheel. The authors contend that the feature should be used more for assistance rather than total autonomy. Lowy covers transportation issues for the Associated Press. Krisher is an auto writer for the Associated Press with more than ten years covering auto-related issues.

"Tesla Driver Killed in Crash While Using Car's 'Autopilot,'" by Joan Lowy and Tom Krisher, Phys.org, June 30, 2016.

AS YOU READ, CONSIDER THE FOLLOWING QUESTIONS:

1. As reported in this viewpoint, how many miles of Autopilot operation had been completed before this first accident occurred?
2. According to Tesla, what responsibility does a driver have when using Autopilot?
3. As reported by the authors, what is the National Highway Traffic Safety Administration (NHTSA) doing for autonomous cars?

The first US fatality using self-driving technology took place in May when the driver of a Tesla S sports car operating the vehicle's "Autopilot" automated driving system died after a collision with a truck in Florida, federal officials said Thursday.

The government is investigating the design and performance of Tesla's system.

Preliminary reports indicate the crash occurred when a tractor-trailer rig made a left turn in front of the Tesla at an intersection of a divided highway where there was no traffic light, the National Highway Traffic Safety Administration said. The Tesla driver died due to injuries sustained in the crash, which took place May 7 in Williston, Florida, the agency said. The city is southwest of Gainesville.

First Known Death

Tesla said on its website that neither the driver nor the Autopilot noticed the white side of the trailer, which was perpendicular to the Model S, against the brightly lit sky, and neither applied the brakes.

"The high ride height of the trailer combined with its positioning across the road and the extremely rare circumstances of the impact caused the Model S to pass under the trailer," the company said. The windshield of the Model S collided with the bottom of the trailer.

By the time firefighters arrived, the wreckage of the Tesla—with its roof sheared off completely—was hundreds of feet from the crash site where it had come to rest in a nearby yard, assistant chief Danny Wallace of the Williston Fire Department told The Associated Press. The driver was pronounced dead, "Signal Seven" in the local

Will self-driving cars eliminate or increase the number of road accidents? While the concept of such cars is appealing, safety is an important goal.

firefighters' jargon, and they respect-
fully covered the wreckage and waited
for crash investigators to arrive.

The company said this was the
first known death in over 130 million
miles of Autopilot operation. It said
the NHTSA investigation is a preliminary inquiry to determine whether the
system worked as expected.

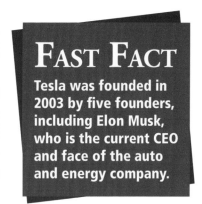

FAST FACT

Tesla was founded in
2003 by five founders,
including Elon Musk,
who is the current CEO
and face of the auto
and energy company.

An Assist Feature

Tesla says that before Autopilot can be used, drivers have to acknowledge that the system is an "assist feature" that requires a driver to
keep both hands on the wheel at all times. Drivers are told they need
to "maintain control and responsibility for your vehicle" while using
the system, and they have to be prepared to take over at any time, the
statement said.

Autopilot makes frequent checks, making sure the driver's hands
are on the wheel, and it gives visual and audible alerts if hands aren't
detected, and it gradually slows the car until a driver responds, the
statement said.

Tesla conceded that the Autopilot feature is not perfect, but said
in the statement that it's getting better all the time. "When used
in conjunction with driver oversight, the data is unequivocal that
Autopilot reduces driver workload and results in a statistically significant improvement in safety," the company said.

The Tesla driver was identified as Joshua D. Brown, 40, of Canton,
Ohio. He was a former Navy SEAL who owned a technology com-
pany, according an obituary posted online by the *Murrysville Star* in
Pennsylvania.

Tesla's founder, Elon Musk, expressed "our condolences for the
tragic loss" in a tweet late Thursday.

NHTSA's Office of Defects is handling the investigation. The
opening of the preliminary evaluation shouldn't be construed as
a finding that the government believes the Model S is defective,
NHTSA said in a statement.

Eliminating Human Error

The Tesla death comes as NHTSA is taking steps to ease the way onto the nation's roads for self-driving cars, an anticipated sea-change in driving where Tesla has been on the leading edge. Self-driving cars have been expected to be a boon to safety because they'll eliminate human errors. Human error is responsible for about 94 percent of crashes.

NHTSA Administrator Mark Rosekind is expected to release guidance to states next month defining the federal role in regulating the vehicles versus the state role, and suggesting what laws and regulations states might want to adopt. Federal officials and automakers say they want to avoid a patchwork of state and local laws that could hinder adoption of the technology.

Most automakers are investing heavily in the technology, which is expected to become more widely available over the next five years. Like the Model S, the first generation of self-driving cars is expected to be able to travel only on highways and major well-marked roadways with a driver ready to take over. But fully self-driving vehicles are forecast to become available in the next 10 to 20 years.

Musk has been bullish about Autopilot, even as Tesla warns owners the feature is not for all conditions and is not sophisticated enough for the driver to check out.

This spring, Musk said the feature reduced the probability of having an accident by 50 percent, without detailing his calculations. In January, he said that Autopilot is "probably better than a person right now."

One of Tesla's advantages over competitors is that its thousands of cars feed real-world performance information back to the company, which can then fine-tune the software that runs Autopilot.

Other companies have invested heavily in developing prototypes of fully self-driving cars, in which a human would be expected to have minimal involvement—or none at all. Alphabet Inc.'s X lab has reported the most crashes of its Google self-driving cars, though it also has the most testing on public roads. In only one did the company acknowledge that its car was responsible for the crash, when a retrofitted Lexus SUV hit a public bus in Northern California on Valentine's Day.

EVALUATING THE AUTHORS' ARGUMENTS:

In this viewpoint, Joan Lowy and Tom Krisher write about the first US fatality involving self-driving technology. Tesla admitted that the autopilot feature was not completely autonomous and that drivers still need to maintain control of the vehicle. Give two suggestions how Tesla could make sure that buyers of its self-driving cars understand the limitations of current Autopilot systems.

Self-Driving Cars Can Be Hacked

Siraj Ahmed Shaikh and Madeline Cheah

"Once hackers get into your internet-connected car, they could disable the air bags, brakes, door locks and even steal the vehicle."

In the following viewpoint, Siraj Ahmed Shaikh and Madeline Cheah argue that the fact that self-driving cars are not secure can pose a threat to the safety of passengers. The authors alert readers about how it is relatively easy for hackers to get into the car's system through the internet and cause all sorts of damage, including taking control of the steering and brake system as well as stealing the car. Shaikh and Cheah conclude the article by reassuring readers that the industry is working on ways to combat these security issues. Shaikh is a professor in systems security at the Centre for Transport and Mobility Research at Coventry University. Cheah works in cybersecurity, specifically that of vehicles and the associated software, in collaboration with HORIBA MIRA, through a graduate program at Coventry University.

1. Identify the three main reasons why cars are becoming vulnerable to cyber attacks, as reported by the authors.
2. According to the viewpoint, what is a "connected car"?
3. As stated by the authors, what is one way that car companies are trying to guard against cyber attacks on cars?

Once hackers get into your internet-connected car, they could disable the air bags, brakes, door locks and even steal the vehicle. That's the finding of researchers who recently uncovered a flaw in the way the different components of a connected car talk to each other. Their work follows several demonstrations of researchers remotely hacking into and taking control of cars, including one that led to a worldwide recall of one connected model of Jeep.

None of these hacks have yet been demonstrated with regular vehicles on the road. But they show how cyber security is becoming a big challenge to the car industry, especially as vehicles incorporate more and more driverless technology. It has even worried the UK government enough to release a set of guidelines for the sector. These emphasize the need for companies to work together to build resilient vehicles whose security can be managed throughout their lifetime. But what can actually be done to ensure that as cars effectively become computers on wheels they are kept safe from hackers?

A Treasure Trove of Data

There are three main reasons why cars are becoming vulnerable to cyber attacks, and these trends have also made security more challenging to design and test. First, the different systems that make up a car are increasingly designed to work together to improve their efficiency and so they all need to be able to communicate, as well as being connected to a central control. Adding autonomous systems that make cars partly or fully self-driving means the vehicles also have to connect to other cars and infrastructure on the road.

Hackers can take control of your car while you're driving it or even steal it. Building security into the design of self-driving vehicles is essential.

But this opens up what was traditionally a closed system to outside, possibly malicious influences. For example, we've seen demonstrations of attacks using cars' Bluetooth, WiFi and radio frequency (RF) on passive key entry systems, which all create possible entry points for hackers.

Second, more features and functionality in cars means more software and more complexity. A single vehicle can now use millions of lines of code, put together in different ways in different components from different manufacturers. This makes it hard for security testers to know where to look, and hard for auditors to check a car complies with the rules. If the software recently used by Volkswagen to circumvent emissions limits had been a malicious virus, it may have taken months or years to find the problem.

Finally, the volume and variety of the data and content stored and used in a vehicle is ever increasing. For example, a car's multimedia

GPS system could contain contact addresses, information about the driver's usual routes and, in the future, even financial data. Such a hoard of information would be very attractive to cyber criminals.

One of the best ways to protect connected cars from this growing threat is by building security into the design of the vehicles. This means, for example, ensuring that there are no conflicts, errors or misconfigurations in individual components. Fully assembled cars should be tested more rigorously to ensure the final product lives up against security hacks, using methods such as penetration testing, whereby systems are purposefully attacked to expose flaws. This in turn would mean better tools and standards that would force everyone in the industry to factor in security right from the start.

The next big challenge is likely to be designing vehicles that match security with safety. As self-driving technology evolves to use more artificial intelligence and deep learning techniques, we will be relying on yet more software to control our cars and make decisions on safety grounds like human drivers would. This will make it even more important that the cars are secure so that they also protect drivers' safety.

Industry Response

The industry is slowly but steadily responding to the growing threat of cyber attacks. Aside from government regulations, the US Society of Automotive Engineers (SAE), has introduced its own set of guidelines that show how cyber security can be treated like other safety threats when designing a car. There are also efforts to make drivers more able to protect their vehicles, for example by warning them in car manuals against plugging in unknown devices.

In the longer run, the biggest challenge is simply getting the car industry to coordinate more. The sector is very competitive at every level, and companies rely on the latest autonomous and connected technologies to set themselves apart and win new customers.

This rivalry means that companies are reluctant to share intelligence about cyber threats and vulnerabilities or work together to develop more secure designs. To make cars truly secure we'll need to see the industry change gear.

EVALUATING THE AUTHORS' ARGUMENTS:

In this viewpoint, Siraj Ahmed Shaikh and Madeline Cheah discuss the various security issues that come along with self-driving cars, with the biggest issue being that they can be hacked. How could measures to protect against cyber attacks in cars also prevent carjackings?

Autonomous Cars May Lead to Vehicle Sharing

Ben Schonberger and Steve Gutmann

"Self-driving technology could cause a societal shift away from private car ownership and toward vehicle sharing."

In the following viewpoint, Ben Schonberger and Steve Gutmann argue the impact that self-driving cars may have on the auto industry, city economics, and the environment. The belief is that autonomous technology will lead to fewer people purchasing their own cars and more people sharing their vehicles with others. There is also a belief that self-driving cars would be more efficient and would spend less time idling or driving, which would cut down on emissions and pollution. Schonberger is a land use planner at Winterbrook Planning. Gutmann serves as a consultant with an interest in various forms of networked transportation.

AS YOU READ, CONSIDER THE FOLLOWING QUESTIONS:

1. Identify three benefits that cities might experience from on-demand cars as reported in the viewpoint.
2. According to the authors, who might benefit from driverless technology?
3. What are the possible negative impacts of this technology as suggested in the article?

One prediction for a future that includes self-driving cars is that more of us will share, rather than own, vehicles.

Cars that drive themselves seemed like science fiction just a few years ago, but recent demonstration projects have shown that the technology is already here. Self-driving car technology, pioneered by Google, has advanced so quickly that its ubiquitous presence on city streets is now simply a matter of time. Boosters say that mass-market autonomous cars are only 3 to 5 years away; others estimate at least 10 years. No one doubts they are coming.

But ideas about how these cars will affect cities and the environment seem to be stuck in the past. People think of self-driving, or driverless, technology as something added on to personal cars. Personal cars, however, spend 95 percent of their time parked, going nowhere, and waiting until they are needed. It's more likely that city dwellers will view this technology as a service, like calling for a taxi. In principle, an on-demand car service could offer the door-to-door mobility of car travel without the fixed costs and hassles of owning a car.

Self-driving technology could cause a societal shift away from private car ownership and toward vehicle sharing. Widespread use of on-demand car services would result in fewer vehicles, which would then transform urban land use. Cities could reap significant benefits: fewer parking lots, more relatively dense, walkable neighborhoods, cleaner air, and reduced carbon emissions.

Car-sharing programs like car2go offer spontaneous, one-way, pay-by-the-minute rentals within a prescribed service area. Members use a smartphone app to locate a nearby car, get to it, swipe a card to unlock, and drive to their destination. When they get there, users park the car at the curb and walk away, leaving it available for the next user.

Now imagine a mash-up of this popular model and Google's self-driving car technology. The car-sharing fleet could be retrofitted with self-driving navigation systems. (Let's call the hypothetical startup company "Car2Google." Of course, other car-sharing services like Zipcar or even traditional rental car companies could jump into the game.) Layering self-driving technology onto this system would allow people to order a car from a fleet and have the car pick them up. It's a taxi service without the drivers. Users would summon a car with their phone and wait comfortably indoors. The car would call or text them as it approaches. Users would then hop in, talk on the phone, or nap while the car drives to their destination. Once there, they can just walk away. The service charges their credit card an amount based on the time or length of the trip.

In addition to improving car sharing for the 1.7 million people who already use such a service, driverless technology would expand the appeal to a wide range of people, including those who:

- are too young to drive;
- are too old or infirm to drive;
- have had their license suspended;
- are too drunk or stoned to drive safely.

Parents could safely deliver their children to or from soccer practice or play dates simply by ordering a vehicle for them. Elderly people who should no longer be behind the wheel and disabled people who cannot drive would still have mobility, with the travel arrangements made independently or by caregivers. And everyone would benefit from impaired late-night revelers having a safe way to get home.

Does this sound like a fantasy? Rapid changes just in the last year bring this idea a lot closer to reality.

- Driverless technology is becoming more reliable, safer, and cheaper. Google's six autonomous vehicles being tested in California have already logged more than 300,000 miles without incident. A Romanian teenager and an Israeli company have created low-cost versions of a self-driving car.
- Auto manufacturers are running to keep up. General Motors, Ford, Volkswagen/Audi, Nissan, Toyota, BMW, Volvo, Cadillac, and Mercedes-Benz (which, like car2go, is a subsidiary of Daimler) have all begun testing these systems.
- Legal barriers are falling away. Nevada, California, and Florida have enacted laws allowing the use of self-driving vehicles for testing purposes. A similar law was introduced in Oregon in early 2013, but it died in the legislature.
- Car sharing is an established program ready for technological breakthroughs. The popular car2go already serves 18 cities in North America and Europe. It is adding more cities all the time.

Self-driving vehicles would vastly increase the efficiency of car sharing. When not being used, cars would drive toward potential users instead of sitting idle and waiting for users to come to them. Instead of having workers going out into the field to service the fleet, cars could go to a central location when on-board sensors or user feedback recommend maintenance. A vehicle would take itself offline, drive itself to be washed or have its oil changed, and then put itself back online when ready to pick up another customer.

Driverless technology would also allow for a greener fleet. Urban trips are usually short hops ideally suited to electric vehicles. And when the battery level drops below a certain threshold, an autonomous vehicle could go offline and drive itself to the nearest available inductive charging pad to recharge.

Many households are already giving up their second vehicle—or sometimes even their only one—in favor of a mix of car sharing, bicycling, and using mass transit. A convenient, self-driving shared vehicle service could accelerate this trend. Traditional vehicles would likely still be needed for camping trips or to pick up a load of gravel, for instance, but these specialty vehicles could also be rented, perhaps from the same company.

This scenario of a city buzzing with fleets of self-driving vehicles may sound futuristic, but existing technology can already do everything described here. Automated car technology can also be applied gradually, one element at a time. Commercial airliners and many transit systems are already nearly fully automated.

The legal system and insurance interests are predictably wary of self-driving cars, and it will take time for individuals to grow comfortable with the idea of taking their hands off the wheel and their feet off the pedal. But legalization has already begun in several states, the Internet is rife with remarkable self-driving car videos, surveys show popular acceptance of the idea, and Google's test models have a spotless safety record thus far.

Although the future is murky and the impacts of this system are unclear, if such a service took off, cities could enjoy a wide array of benefits.

Less traffic. Studies have shown that each car-sharing vehicle takes between 9 and 13 privately owned vehicles off the road. When people pay for driving by the trip, they see the real costs; therefore, car-sharing members drive 44 percent less than personal vehicle owners do. Cruising to find parking spots would no longer be an issue, thereby eliminating a third of traffic in some urban areas.

Fewer parking spaces. More than a third of land area in some US cities is dedicated to car storage. If people shift away from personal cars and toward shared vehicles, most of those parking spaces would become unnecessary. Acres of empty parking lots and driveways in desirable locations would open up for more productive uses like housing, playgrounds, or parks. If the change happens quickly, urban land prices could tumble.

Safer streets. People are terrible drivers. Human error causes or contributes to more than 90 percent of car crashes. Getting behind the wheel is the riskiest thing most people do in a day. Self-driving cars would be programmed to never speed, make sudden lane changes, or let drunk or distracted drivers make life-or-death decisions. The lead engineer on Google's project expects driverless cars to sharply reduce crashes of all kinds.

Cost savings. Personal car ownership costs about $9,000 per year. Among young people especially, rates of driving and car ownership are already falling. A convenient car-sharing service that saves money could convince people to sell their cars while allowing them to maintain their same level of mobility.

Environmental benefits. More efficient travel patterns, fewer vehicles, cleaner cars, and less driving overall would lead to better urban air quality and lower carbon emissions. Less land would be paved over for parking, reducing stormwater runoff and heat island effects. These sustainability benefits would be market-driven and would not require government subsidy.

As with any potentially disruptive technology, the benefits might not materialize in the way we predict, and the future might not be as rosy as it seems. Consider the techno-pessimistic future:

More traffic. Economists are quick to point out that people usually consume more of something when it becomes cheaper. If people can sleep or work on their laptops while in a car, perhaps they will drive more and commute even longer distances. We simply don't know how much unmet, latent demand there is for vehicle travel. In addition, trips that previously did not exist would result from new users (children, blind people), people who shift from mass transit, and the self-redistribution of empty vehicles driving to the next user.

Sprawl. Currently, only a small number of workers are super commuters who live an hour or more by car from their jobs. But if technology can eliminate the fatigue and aggravation of driving, more people may choose this lifestyle. The boom of streetcar suburbs in the 1890s and, later, auto-oriented suburbs in the 1940s showed that new modes of transportation have big effects on where people choose to live.

Less safe streets. If fewer cars sit parked and more of them are constantly circulating, streets could become busier. Early testing has been very promising, but self-driving cars have not been set loose on the full range of chaotic real-world conditions such as erratic drivers, snow-covered streets, and software or mechanical glitches.

Job losses. Certain workers lose out in this imagined future. Cab drivers, parking lot attendants, transit workers (who will likely be displaced not only by driverless cars but also driverless buses and trains), car dealers, and repair shops will become less necessary. Other jobs might pop up to replace them, but it is uncertain what they would be.

EVALUATING THE AUTHORS' ARGUMENTS:

In this viewpoint, Ben Schonberger and Steve Gutmann analyze the issue of self-driving cars and the potential merging of this technology with the practice of car sharing. The authors discuss several of the benefits of autonomous vehicles, including the benefit of car sharing. The authors also outline both benefits and problems with the proposed technology. Do you think that this future scenario will be beneficial or not? Support your view with evidence from the article.

Self-Driving Cars Can Be Both Positive and Negative for the Environment

Carolyn Beeler

"Commutes might become longer as driverless cars change where we live."

In the following viewpoint, Carolyn Beeler argues the positives and the negatives of self-driving cars, while largely focusing on how they will affect the environment. Beeler writes that car sharing may increase, and the amount of fuel and energy we use may decrease. However, she also contends that some self-driving cars will be fully electric, thus eliminating gas, emissions, and pollution. Although the author is not sure where autonomous cars will take us, she urges people to start planning for them now in order to be prepared. Beeler is an environmental reporter and producer at the BBC and PRI.

1. According to the viewpoint, what comparison is made about fuel consumption?
2. Identify two possible downsides to this technology as reported by the author.
3. According to Beeler, what does Singapore assume its citizens will do with regard to transportation?

What will self-driving cars mean for the environment? Backers of the technology argue that autonomous vehicles will drive more efficiently than humans do—no more slamming on breaks or gunning it at yellow lights—so they'll save gas and reduce pollution.

But early research reveals a wide range of emissions possibilities for driverless cars.

A 2016 report found that automated vehicles could reduce fuel consumption by as much as 90 percent, or increase it by 200 percent.

"We are on a path to refine those numbers, as are other researchers, because it was quite a startling future," says Ann Schlenker at Argonne National Laboratory in Illinois, one of the Department of Energy–affiliated labs that authored the report.

In a big garage downstairs from Schlenker's office, about half a dozen cars are hooked up to testing equipment. Argonne researchers have found that features already offered in some cars, like adaptive cruise control and automated shifting into electric mode, do save gas.

"All of those early automation features do indeed improve the environmental signature," Schlenker says.

Argonne research has also found that truck "platooning" could improve fuel economy between 8 and 15 percent. Platooning, or driving in tight formation to reduce drag, may be possible with the improved safety features of automated vehicles.

Other features on fully automated cars could reduce fuel consumption even more.

Widespread use of autonomous vehicles could help the environment. However, it is impossible to predict how our lifestyle patterns will adapt to the technology.

This Is the Good News. But There's Bad News Too.

Even if each individual trip becomes more efficient with automation, we may make a lot more trips overall.

With a car as a chauffeur, Schlenker points out that people who don't currently use cars will be able to: like elderly people who can't drive anymore, and kids.

Commutes might become longer as driverless cars change where we live.

"Rather than a 30-minute commute, now you're willing to entertain a 60-minute commute to get cheaper housing because [you] can be productive while the car takes [you] into the office," Schlenker says.

Yet another factor: without human error, the risk of car crashes is predicted to plummet. That's a main selling point for automated vehicles, and it's a great thing for safety, but it might also have a downside. With the risk of crashes greatly reduced, we may have our cars drive us faster and use a lot more gas.

"Some of these future scenarios are very scary," says Jason Rugolo, a program director at ARPA-E, the Energy Department agency that invests in advanced energy technologies.

Rugolo is looking at starting an ARPA-E program funding research into fuel-efficient driverless car designs so these scary future scenarios don't materialize.

"For example, we could invest in autonomous vehicles that are much lighter weight, they could have much better drag coefficients so they look much more like a fish instead of a block moving through the air," Rugolo says.

Heavy safety features like safety cages and big front-ends with crumple zones could be ditched if autonomous vehicles do, in fact, live up to their reputation as super safe.

Will We Share Driverless Cars?

A key part of the futurist narrative of self-driving cars is that they could increase car-sharing and decrease car ownership.

After a car drops you off at work, for example, it could drive other people around all day before picking you up again. If that happens, cars could be better tailored to specific uses.

Sleek, one-person pods could transport commuters to work, and larger multi-seat cars would be used only for weekend trips with the whole family.

"All of these developments could dramatically reduce the amount of energy we use, even if we're driving very fast and very far," Rugolo says.

But these futuristic car designs are just ideas for now, and companies like Uber are currently turning regular cars into self-driving prototypes.

A Massachusetts-based startup called nuTonomy is testing its cars, electric Renaults fitted with sensors, cameras and computer equipment, on the streets of Boston. And it's giving test rides overseas.

"We partnered with a company called Grab, which is kind of the Uber of Singapore," says CEO Karl Iagnemma. "So a customer could hail one of our cars, and if we happen to be on the road at that time, we would pick them up and they could take a ride in a self-driving car."

One day Iagnemma wants to compete with current ride-sharing companies by offering cheaper fares.

Iagnemma is dedicated to using electric cars to decrease his fleet's carbon footprint, but beyond that, he's not quite sure what his business model might mean for pollution.

"One thing that may happen is if you reduce the cost of transportation, people may take more trips because it's cheaper, but it's hard to predict," Iagnemma says.

Government Planners Have a Role to Play

Singapore, where nuTonomy is testing its technology, is a tiny, crowded country that doesn't want more cars clogging its streets—driverless or otherwise.

The city-state is encouraging nuTonomy's self-driving car innovation, and is itself investing in self-driving buses, for a rather counterintuitive reason. Leaders there hope the introduction of driverless cars will actually help Singaporeans drive less.

The Ministry of Transport included self-driving vehicles in its transportation master plan.

"Our plan is that by 2030, 8 in 10 people will be able to walk to the train station," says Lee Chuan Teck, Singapore's deputy secretary of transportation.

For the two in 10 who can't, Lee wants tiny self-driving cars to fill the gap.

"Self-driving pods to bring people from their doorstep to the train station, I think will help encourage more people to take public transport," Lee says.

And Singapore's planners hope that by saving on salary costs with autonomous buses, they'll be able to expand their bus networks to serve new parts of the city.

This future full of self-driving pods and autonomous busses is years away.

But experts say if we don't start planning for it now, driverless cars could land us right where we started: stuck in traffic, surrounded by bad air.

EVALUATING THE AUTHOR'S ARGUMENTS:

In this viewpoint, Carolyn Beeler discusses how self-driving cars may affect the environment. One point the author mentions is that people may be willing to live further from their jobs and have a longer commute since they don't physically need to drive themselves to work. Do you agree with Beeler? Why or why not? Use evidence from the viewpoint to back up your opinion.

Chapter 2

Do Self-Driving Cars Benefit Society?

Can driverless cars eliminate traffic jams on the freeway?

Viewpoint 1

Self-Driving Cars Will Ease Congestion and Parking

Ian Adams

"So long as an autonomous vehicle is safer than a traditionally directed vehicle, the Chinese government appears satisfied."

In the following viewpoint, Ian Adams argues that self-driving cars have great potential for increasing safety because they will eliminate heavy traffic. The author focuses on the traffic situation in Beijing, China, one of the densest urban areas in the world. He contends that since China's federal government enjoys unilateral authority, as opposed to the federal and state government levels of the United States, regulation of automated vehicles will be much more expedient in China. The author predicts that innovation and development in the United States will be hampered due to struggles over government safety regulations. Adams is associate vice president of state affairs with the R Street Institute. He also is involved in matters related to next-generation transportation.

AS YOU READ, CONSIDER THE FOLLOWING QUESTIONS:
1. How many people in China are killed in road accidents every year, according to the viewpoint?
2. In what year does the automotive engineer cited in the viewpoint predict autonomous urban use of self-driving cars?
3. What does the author suggest China do to take advantage of the lead it may have over the United States?

I n Beijing, a young car culture is going through teething pains. The pressure of urban density, in combination with growing demand for personal transportation in an ever-more-affluent city, has the capital of the People's Republic aching for relief.

It's thus no wonder that a generation of Chinese people see driving as a pain. Unlike car culture in the United States, which came of age during a romantic period of road trips, China's car culture has come of age in a period of congestion.

China's next great leap in transportation cannot come soon enough, not only as a matter of commuter convenience, but as a matter of necessity. Ring roads and surface streets flush with cars at all hours have become the bustling capital's economic choke point. A 2014 study by Peking University estimated that congestion is costing Beijing alone roughly $11.3 billion per year. More importantly, the World Health Organization estimates that 200,000 people are killed in China in road accidents every year.

Chinese Government Pushing for Innovation

The Chinese government—specifically, the Ministry of Industry and Information Technology—is keenly aware of these issues. To its credit, it believes autonomous vehicles will be an essential part of the solution. The ministry has signaled that it intends to mandate a series of technical and development benchmarks that are to be reached by certain dates.

Li Keqiang, an automotive engineering professor at Tsinghua University who is affiliated with the ministry, has received wide coverage for his claim that a draft roadmap for the introduction of

Self-driving cars have the opportunity to transform society for the better. It is believed that China will be at the forefront of such changes.

self-driving cars for highway use within three to five years, and autonomous urban use by 2025, is likely to be released later this year.

A series of international conferences have been held in China this year already to discuss the country's approach to autonomous vehicles. In April, Beijing hosted a conference of industry CEOs, an international auto show and the Global Smart Car Summit at the Global Mobile Internet Conference. The stakeholders in attendance are keenly aware that while developments will be made in the private sector, China's regulation of autonomous vehicles is a matter of central planning.

The United States Could Fall Behind

Unlike the United States, where authority over autonomous vehicle development and standards is split between the states and the federal government, China's industry enjoys the benefits of broad-scale coordination. In the near term, this will likely mean that China will not suffer through the same regulatory frustration that will slow the rollout of similar technology here.

What's more, China has pent-up demand for new vehicles and the ability and will to undertake large infrastructure projects. While US regulators are pursing unrealistically onerous safety standards that could actually stunt widespread adopting of the technology, China is approaching safety as a relative matter. So long as an autonomous vehicle is safer than a traditionally directed vehicle, the Chinese government appears satisfied.

But in the long term, in the event that technical coordination becomes too granular, China could face a Minitel-like disaster of hitherto unknown proportions. The way that China can avoid such an outcome will be to embrace the raft of foreign firms with expertise in the field that are increasingly frustrated by the obstacles presented to them in the United States. Doing so will mean taking the hard step of moving away from mandated domestic communications monopolies (like Chinese firm BeiDou on satellite navigation), but the technical benefits of such a development likely would be tremendous.

To be clear, centrally planning regulatory liberalization is hardly ideal. But given the political realities that prevail in China, in the case of autonomous-vehicle development, it stands to bring a world of good to the Middle Kingdom.

EVALUATING THE AUTHOR'S ARGUMENTS:

In this viewpoint, Ian Adams discusses how government regulation can either help or hinder technological innovation. Can you think of examples where this has happened with another type of technology?

Self-Driving Cars Could Lead to Increased Congestion in Our Cities

"Congestion will be bad enough to be ruining people's lives, wrecking the urban environment, strangling public transit, worsening climate change, and so on."

Jarrett Walker

In the following viewpoint, Jarrett Walker analyzes a report concerning driverless cars. Walker argues that the benefits and downsides of this technology will depend on the method of car ownership, particularly in traditionally trafficky urban areas. He poses a scenario that demonstrates how, contrary to many opinions, widespread autonomous car ownership could result in an increase in congestion. Walker is an international consultant who wites about issues of public transit and transportation design, including the book *Human Transit: How Clearer Thinking About Public Transit Can Enrich Our Communities and Our Lives.*

"Self-Driving Cars: A Coming Congestion Disaster?," Human Transit, November 25, 2015. Reprinted by permission.

AS YOU READ, CONSIDER THE FOLLOWING QUESTIONS:
1. According to Walker's analysis, what issue will affect driverless car technology?
2. This viewpoint sketches out a probable scenario that increases congestion. Why might this happen?
3. Who or what will alleviate the potential problem of congestion, according to this report?

We're starting to see professional reports echoing long-standing concerns about how driverless cars will affect our cities. This new one from KPMG, in particular, is getting a lot of press. It's actually a focus group study about the transport desires of different generations, but it confirms the thought experiments that many of us have already been laying out for a while.

Much depends on whether these cars are owned or spontaneously hired like taxis, Uber, and Lyft. A taxi model is definitely better in its congestion impacts, but that doesn't mean it will happen. The ownership model is closer to the status quo, and the status quo always has enormous power. Driverless taxis will not always be available on demand, especially in suburban and rural areas, so a legitimate fear of being stranded will make people in those areas prefer the security of having a car just for them. And of course, that's just the effect of rational concerns about relying on taxis. Less rational desires for car ownership, as an expression of identity or symbol of liberty, will also not vanish overnight.

A Nightmare Scenario

This leads to a nightmare scenario that University of Washington's Mark Hollenbeck laid out in our recent *Seattle Times* panel. Paraphrasing Mark: A suburban father rides his driverless car to work, maybe dropping his daughter off at school. But rather than park the car downtown, he simply tells it to drive back home to his house in the suburbs. During the day, it runs some other errands for his family. At 3 pm, it goes to the school to bring his daughter home

There is a possibility that driverless cars will lead to more trips and more congestion if they are used as personal chauffeurs.

or chauffeur her to after-school activities. Then it's time for it to drive back into the city to pick up Dad from work. But then, on a lark, Dad decides to go shopping at a downtown department store after work, so he tells his car to just circle the block for an hour while he shops, before finally hailing it to go home.

This is really easy and obvious behavior for a driverless car owner. It reduces the number of cars someone needs to own, and reduces pressure on inner city parking, but would cause an explosive growth in vehicle trips, and thus in congestion (not to mention emissions and other impacts). Just the commute behavior doubles car volumes, because the car now makes a two-way trip for each direction of the commute, instead of just one. And if everyone shopping downtown has a car circling the block waiting for them, well, that level of congestion will far exceed what's generated by cars circling for parking today. It could pretty well shut down the city.

This is the good old problem of induced demand, which is what happens when you make a resource available at an artificially low price—as we do with most urban roads today. If you don't pay the true cost of something in money, you will pay it in time, and that's what congestion is. (It's also why in the old Soviet Union, people spent hours waiting to buy bread: Soviet price controls made the price too low to compensate the suppliers, so there wasn't enough bread, so everyone waited in line. Congestion—waiting in line to use an underpriced road—works the same way.)

Possible Solutions

Pricing of some kind will be the solution, but we tend to do this only when things get really bad. Notice how bad congestion has to be today before solutions like toll lanes and transit lanes are finally accepted as necessary.

As always, the very worst scenario won't happen, but some really bad ones still can. If the economic functioning of downtown is too badly impaired by driverless cars circling the block waiting for their owners, the government will intervene to save the economy, as it always does, probably with some kind of downtown street pricing on the London or Singapore model. But this only happens when congestion threatens the economy. That's a very high bar. Long before that point, congestion will be bad enough to be ruining people's lives, wrecking the urban environment, strangling public transit, worsening climate change, and so on.

As always, the scary thing about congestion is how bad people (and therefore governments) allow it to get before they start making different choices to avoid it. The level of congestion we (justifiably) complain about is much lower than the level that we choose to tolerate, and this is the real reason for pessimism about how bad congestion could potentially get, if driverless car ownership—like cars today—are so massively underpriced even in the context of high urban demand.

EVALUATING THE AUTHOR'S ARGUMENTS:

In this viewpoint, Jarrett Walker cites evidence that points to an increase in future road and driving congestion caused by privately owned driverless cars. What do you think could change the common mind-set in the United States concerning individually owned and used cars?

How Self-Driving Cars Can Benefit the Environment

Roddy Scheer

"To ensure that autonomous vehicles deliver economic, energy security and environmental benefits, we will need supporting policies targeted at those objectives."

In the following viewpoint, Roddy Scheer analyzes statistics from several reports pointing to the positive effects of driverless cars on the environment. From "platoon" or closely driving vehicles, to computer assisted ride sharing which would drastically reduce the number of cars on the roads, proponents of the new technology are excited about the possible benefits. In addition, Scheer includes information from researchers who warn about the possible downsides to the new technology. Scheer is a journalist specializing in environmental issues and produces EarthTalk Q&A, a weekly syndicated column dedicated to helping people understand complex environmental issues.

AS YOU READ, CONSIDER THE FOLLOWING QUESTIONS:

1. What are the two ways self-driving cars can benefit the environment?
2. How could self-driving cars hurt energy efficiency?
3. What precautions should be taken as this technology is developed?

"Self-Driving Cars Could Be Great for the Environment," by Roddy Scheer, Earth Action Network, Inc., December 10, 2016. Reprinted by permission.

Driverless cars could benefit the environment, provided industry standards and government policies work together with that goal in mind.

You know the future is here when you see that the car beside you at a red light has nobody at the helm. That's already happening in California where a few companies (Uber, Google, Apple, Tesla) have begun testing autonomous vehicles on the open road—albeit with human drivers at the ready in case anything goes wrong. Meanwhile, the major automakers have begun integrating autonomous driving technologies (blind spot detection, GPS mapping, assisted parking, etc.) into existing models, and will surely offer their own fully self-driving cars once lawmakers qualify them as street legal, maybe as early as 2018.

Proponents say that not only will driverless cars make our roads safer (as they can sense walkers, bikers, other cars and road infrastructure to avoid collisions), but will also be a boon to the environment. Zia Wadud, who co-authored a study released earlier this year assessing the travel, energy and carbon impacts of autonomous vehicles, says the widespread adoption of the technology could reduce energy consumption significantly.

"Automated vehicles can interact with each other and drive very closely as a 'platoon,'" reports Wadud. "This can reduce the total energy consumption of road transport by 4% to 25%, because vehicles which follow closely behind each other face less air resistance." Beyond the platoon benefit, driverless cars can also shave another 25 percent off overall automotive energy consumption through more efficient computer-assisted ride optimization.

Yet another environmental benefit could be fewer cars on the road altogether. "Your car could give you a lift to work in the morning and then give a lift to someone else in your family—or, for that matter, to anyone else: After delivering you to your destination, it doesn't sit idle in a parking lot for 20-plus hours every day," report MIT researchers Matthew Claudel and Carlo Ratti in a recent McKinsey.com article. "By combining ride sharing with car sharing ... it would be possible to take every passenger to his or her destination at the time they need to be there, with 80 percent fewer cars." They conclude that clearing four of five cars from the road would have "momentous consequences" for our cities regarding pollution, traffic, efficiency, and parking.

But Jason Bordoff of Columbia University's Center on Global Energy Policy argues in *The Wall Street Journal* that driverless cars hurt overall energy efficiency by undermining public transit: "If you can work, watch a movie or sleep while in the car, perhaps you will take a car rather than public transportation or be more likely to drive for long trips." He adds that autonomous vehicles also "significantly expand the universe of potential drivers" bringing more people (and cars) onto the road and possibly increasing total vehicle miles travelled overall. "Even car-sharing services could increase energy demand if the ease and convenience pulls people away from mass transit, walking or biking and into cars."

Bordoff remains optimistic that autonomous vehicles can provide a net gain for society and the environment, but only if we are careful about how we implement the technology. "To ensure that autonomous vehicles deliver economic, energy security and environmental benefits, we will need supporting policies targeted at those objectives, such as increased fuel-economy standards, investments in public transportation infrastructure, and R&D in alternative vehicle technologies."

For his part, Wadud agrees with Bordoff that driverless cars could actually be bad for the environment depending on how things shake out. "Let's not be blinded by the driverless cars by saying they can solve everything—know that there could be risks and be careful about them," he says. "That said, I do hope that driverless cars will encourage car sharing and help reduce our energy use and carbon emissions. However, what will happen in reality remains to be seen."

EVALUATING THE AUTHOR'S ARGUMENTS:

In this viewpoint, Roddy Scheer cites evidence from several studies suggesting that self-driving cars can potentially be a boon for the environment. Construct an argument to convince someone of this viewpoint, using information from this and the previous viewpoint.

Autonomous Cars Will Result in Job Loss

Joel Lee

"In total, that's a little over 4 million American jobs put at risk due to the coming revolution in self-driving cars—more than 1% of the country."

In the following viewpoint, Joel Lee argues that a great number of current jobs will be lost because of the upcoming technological shift to driverless cars. Lee outlines the types of jobs that may be lost in the United States and presents statistics showing the approximate numbers of individuals who could lose their jobs. The author then contrasts the lost jobs and lost wages against the hoped-for benefits that autonomous vehicles might bring. Lee is an editor and writer for MakeUseOf with a bachelor's degree in computer science.

AS YOU READ, CONSIDER THE FOLLOWING QUESTIONS:
1. According to Joel Lee, what is the one drawback of self-driving cars?
2. Identify three areas of job loss, as stated in the viewpoint.
3. What does the author claim about the long-term gains of autonomous cars?

Truck drivers will be hit hard by the development of autonomous vehicles.

The self-driving car is technology's biggest gift to civilization since the birth of the Internet. It'll be a few decades before driverless cars become the norm, but when that day comes, it will be glorious. Robot cars will restore mobility to the young, elderly, and disabled. They'll make travel cheaper and safer. In short, they're going to change the world.

This impending revolution comes with one huge drawback: robot cars are going to destroy a lot of jobs.

With companies like Tesla already pushing for autonomous features as early as this coming summer, the threat against American jobs is immediate. But just how many jobs will be lost? And is this economic loss justified? The answers may surprise you.

Which Jobs Are at Risk, Exactly?

Not long ago, the first self-driving truck was released into the wild. Freightliner's Inspiration, with its ceremonial license plate of AU 010, is the biggest milestone to be hit since the autonomous vehicle discussion began. It's only legal in Nevada at the moment, and it has a human driver as backup, but it's a monumental step just the same.

But the Inspiration is not a good sign for current truck drivers in the United States. According to the Bureau of Labor Statistics, there were approximately 1.6 million American truck drivers in 2014 earning a mean income of $42,000. That's more than half a percent of the country, and $67 billion dollars in income—about 0.3% of the US GDP.

These new trucks aren't completely autonomous yet, but the technology is going to get there sooner rather than later. And when that day arrives, those truck drivers will need to find something else to do. When you include delivery truck operators, which numbered around 800,000 in 2014, we end up with 2.4 million people who may be out of a job in the next decade or two.

But the bigger topic of conversation when it comes to self-driving cars and their impact? Service drivers. Mainly we're talking about taxi drivers—and more recently, Uber drivers—but also included in the conversation are people like bus drivers.

As autonomous vehicle technology improves, it's easy to imagine a world where these vehicles have no need for a human operator. This would leave the following people jobless: 180,000 taxi drivers, 160,000 Uber drivers, 500,000 school bus drivers, and 160,000 transit bus drivers, for a grand total of 1 million jobs.

And if we extrapolate a bit and throw in a dash of speculation, we can look at the potential impact on peripheral jobs that don't involve direct driving but do provide services to modern day consumer drivers. For example, auto body repair shops.

While driverless cars are nowhere near perfect in terms of safety, they are undoubtedly safer than the average American driver. Over 6 years of public testing, Google's vehicles have only been in 11 minor accidents, and if Google's reports are trustworthy, none of those accidents were caused by the autonomous vehicle.

A study by McKinsey & Company predicts that, in a future where all cars are driverless, we could see a crash rate reduction of up to 90 percent. Lower accident rates would lead to less frequent visits to auto body repair shops, and that would leave a good portion of the 445,000 auto body repairers without a job.

Other peripherally-impacted jobs could include street meter maids, parking lot attendants, gas station attendants, rental car agencies, and more. Not all of these would lose their jobs entirely, but it's hard to imagine that these industries wouldn't be drastically affected, which could affect up to 220,000 more workers.

In total, that's a little over 4 million American jobs put at risk due to the coming revolution in self-driving cars—more than 1% of the country. Do note that this change will tend [to] result in reemployment rather than unemployment, leading to an overall boost in economic productivity, provided the economy continues to expand.

The Economic Benefits of Self-Driving Cars

Now that we've determined how many potential jobs are at risk, let's look at the potential benefits that we can enjoy once autonomous cars become the norm. Will these benefits justify those lost jobs? I'll illustrate what we stand to gain, but only you can decide whether the trade will be worth it.

As mentioned earlier, the McKinsey prediction is that a society of self-driving cars could see a reduction in crash rates up to 90 percent. For the individual, this means less money spent on car repairs, maintenance, and health bills related to automotive accidents—which is estimated to be around $180 billion per year.

On a wider scale, we get fewer accidents when transporting cargo over long distances, so companies save money on lost goods. There's also a slight safety increase since fuel tankers and other volatile vehicles are less prone to crash and burn, but admittedly the gains here may not be significant.

Going back to individual benefits, many regions might move away from the "one car per person" mentality that we currently possess, especially in urban environments. Imagine this: whenever you need a car, you open an app and request one, and it's there in a few minutes. Uber is already faster than an ambulance in cities like London. Robot cars can probably get that number smaller. When you get to your destination, there's no need to find parking—the car simply drives away.

Without needing to own our own vehicles anymore, we'd save on gas, maintenance, parking, and insurance costs.

More remarkably, imagine a scenario in which all of these cars were hooked into a singular network. In essence, cars would talk to one another wirelessly as they traveled, and this kind of hivemind would be a huge step towards more efficient driving. People going to the same places could be pooled, sending buses along popular routes, and smart-cars for one-off trips. Electric cars could be used more easily, since they could charge themselves without needing to inconvenience a person. All of this amounts to huge savings. Using autonomous vehicles could wind up costing only a few cents per mile.

A practical example of this kind of hivemind network would be the case of inner city parking. In places like New York, it's almost impossible to find parking because we all want to park as close to our destination as possible. With autonomous cars, that's no longer necessary. The car can immediately go help someone else when you're done with it. No more waiting around depreciating and using up space. How many hours of your life have been wasted in search of a place to park? Now you can arrive at your destination, step out, and go on with your day—the car will do the same.

Another practical example of the automotive hivemind: traffic efficiency. Did you know that your vehicle's fuel economy rating is based on optimal conditions? If you aren't driving like a perfect robot, you aren't getting anywhere near the fuel economy that you think you are.

For example, the most fuel-efficient way to drive is the "pulse and glide method," which involves a rhythmic alternating between acceleration and coasting. Anything less than that and you're wasting gas. Gas-powered autonomous cars can be programmed with optimal driving behavior, which saves on gas.

But more importantly, optimal driving behavior leads to minimal congestion. Did you know that many traffic jams occur simply due to human inefficiency?

A study by INRIX found that the average American and European driver wastes about 111 hours in gridlock every year. What would you do with an extra 111 hours? With driverless cars, gridlock could be a thing of the past.

What else could we get by cutting humans out of the driving equation?

Perhaps the biggest benefit of the driverless car is that they don't suffer from human flaws. Machines have no need to sleep, which means around-the-clock operation of vehicles, but it also means that they aren't burdened by drowsiness. That's an additional point for the "autonomous cars are safer" column.

Another cost that passes down to the customer: insurance premiums. Insurance rates are calculated based on risk. Since we've already established that driverless cars are significantly safer than the average human driver, insurance costs will plummet. Plus, most of those costs will shift to manufacturers and operators of said cars, leaving us free of that burden.

There are so many more benefits to explore, but I'll end with one that's particularly poignant in light of Tesla's recent advancements in battery technology: the fact that driverless cars are more friendly for the environment.

Most of the aforementioned benefits are about cost savings and gas efficiency: less gridlock, less idling, less searching for parking, and more use of electric vehicles? If we follow that thread, the natural conclusion is that improved efficiency leads to reduced carbon emissions. That's always a good thing.

There are other factors to consider, which you can read about in our defense that autonomous cars are good for the environment.

A New Era Is Around the Corner

The truth is that the advent of a driverless car industry will surely displace more jobs than it will create, but the long-term gains that we'll see as a society far outweigh the short-term growing pains and inconveniences. The economic, environmental, and human benefits are astounding. I truly believe that this is one of the situations where the loss of jobs is a valid sacrifice for the greater good of society.

Would I be singing the same tune if self-writing robots were also on the horizon, threatening my own job? If they offered the same kind of economic value and social benefits as self-driving cars, you bet. Self-driving cars are simply too good to pass up.

EVALUATING THE AUTHOR'S ARGUMENTS:

In this viewpoint, Joel Lee makes a case for autonomous vehicles. He analyzes several areas of job loss he believes will occur and argues that in the end it will be for the good of society. Do you agree with Lee? Why or why not? Support your opinions with facts from this viewpoint.

Self-Driving Cars Will Increase Fuel Efficiency

Tao Lin

"Cars can improve functions that will decrease fuel waste, like maps, automatic braking, [and] accident prevention devices."

In the following viewpoint, Tao Lin reports on a topic concerning self-driving cars that is raised less often than other issues—that of fuel efficiency. Lin provides numerous examples that illustrate where the habits of human drivers cause marked decreases in fuel efficiency. Many of these, he argues, can be corrected by improved software in autonomous vehicles. Self-driving cars have the potential to measurably cut down on waste. Lin wrote this viewpoint for Movimento, an automotive company.

AS YOU READ, CONSIDER THE FOLLOWING QUESTIONS:

1. According to Lin, what does "waste" mean in the auto industry?
2. Identify three driving habits that contribute to fuel waste, as reported by the author.
3. How does software help the problems of waste, according to the author?

Self-driving cars have the potential to cut down our use of gasoline and reduce waste.

When we think of the self-driving car, and of software developments that make cars more and more autonomous, we tend to focus on the safety aspects, and the resulting convenience. We think about how they will transform the automotive industry and the economics of driving. What isn't talked about as much is how they will impact fuel economy and make cars much more efficient, saving fuel and lowering greenhouse emissions.

When Cars Waste Fuel: The Human Factor

When we talk about waste, we have to define first what we mean. Although transportation makes up 27% of greenhouse gas emissions, those aren't all "wasted." Transportation is a key part of the economy, and of our modern civilization. If you are hungry and eat a hot dog, the food isn't wasted. It is only wasteful if you make more hot dogs than you need. What the auto industry is trying to do is reduce the need for fuel by increasing efficiency and limiting waste.

Limiting waste means first identifying where waste exists. Historically, that meant upgrading with better oil, a cleaner-running engine, and other general improvements so that top performance didn't require as much fuel. Most of yesterday's gas-guzzling muscle cars, as awesome as they are, would be considerably slower than your average, fuel-efficient family sedan today.

But so much fuel waste comes from inefficient driving itself. Starting and stopping wastes fuel. Gunning it at green lights or slamming on the brakes wastes fuel. Driving too fast—above 55 mph—greatly decreases fuel efficiency. Think of how much fuel in your life you have wasted because someone who suddenly remembered they had to turn, blocked traffic by trying to switch lanes and you had to slam on the brakes.

There are broader ways in which we waste fuel, like unneeded trips, lack of carpooling, and even simply getting lost. All of these are part of the same basic and understandable problem: human nature. There isn't a single one of us who doesn't gun it when traffic finally clears, or switch lanes suddenly so we don't miss an exit. This can all change with self-driving cars.

How Self-Driving Cars and Easy Software Updates Can Improve Fuel Efficiency

We've all seen (and maybe even been) the person trying to parallel park who takes 30 attempts, gas and brake, pulling out and in, see-sawing into place. That in and out itself isn't much of a waste, but it adds up. It adds up when doing it again and again, compounded by the millions of people who do it. Right now, we already have cars that can parallel park themselves with negligible or non-existent human assistance. Think of all that wasted gas suddenly not being wasted.

Now take that further, as cars become more autonomous. There won't be sudden lane changes, as the cars on the road will know where they are going, and V2V communication ensures a smooth drive. They won't be blazing over the speed limit, or coming to a sudden, screeching halt when a space they see closes. All traffic will move more efficiently. There will be less wasted rides, as well. A car can pick someone up and drop them off, and then pick up the next person, instead of two people driving two cars. Getting lost will also be a thing of the past.

Even now, with OTA software updates, cars can improve functions that will decrease fuel waste, like maps, automatic braking, accident prevention devices, or infotainment apps that help you find a parking space. We don't even have to wait for 2020 or 2025 for these continual improvements which help with fuel efficiency. Smartphone-based OTA software updates from Movimento can deliver these fuel-efficient updates this generation.

The scale has been tipped toward efficiency. Every automaker knows that is the way of the future, for the planet, and for their business. The automotive industry is full of amazing corporate citizens who are working to make their needed products more efficient. Software updates, and the path to the self-driving car, is a huge part of this new revolution.

EVALUATING THE AUTHOR'S ARGUMENTS:

In this viewpoint, Tao Lin expands on the benefits of self-driving cars by analyzing the topic of fuel efficiency. Lin provides statistics and examples to prove his point, suggesting that this aspect will be a big win on the side of technology. Think about this: If fuel efficiency generally diminishes at speeds greater than 50 mph, why do so many states have speed limits well above that mark?

Self-Driving Cars Can Serve as Valuable Data Collectors for Many Industries

Peter Wells

"There will be many other types of data collected by the car that ... will improve transport services, save lives and make things better in other sectors."

One topic not often discussed in the predictions about how self-driving cars will change our world is the opportunity for invaluable data collection. In the following viewpoint, Peter Wells argues that, aside from many other potential benefits such as fewer accidents and reduced traffic congestion, automated cars will collect and rely on valuable data—such as data about traffic, live weather conditions, accidents, maps, and addresses—that can benefit other industries and sectors as they tackle their own problems. Thus, the data tracked by driverless vehicles should be open but secure. Wells is head of policy at the Open Data Institute.

AS YOU READ, CONSIDER THE FOLLOWING QUESTIONS:
1. How much data per hour does the average modern car generate, according to the viewpoint?
2. What drive-capturing smartphone app does the author use as an example?
3. How can self-driving cars help record and update address listings?

Everyone's talking about automated cars and how they will make it cheaper and easier for us to get from place to place. As well as helping us travel they will change our cities by freeing up space, save lives by reducing the number of driving accidents and lead to the loss of millions of driving jobs with the associated impact on people and communities.

If you're reading this I bet you've heard this talk. If you live in one of the test areas in America, UK, China and etcetera you may even have seen trials. There are skeptics, but I think that people will be able to gradually build ever safer and more automated cars. Once they do many people will choose to use them. Change is coming. Making it easier and cheaper to move around, changing cities, saving lives, removing a type of job are complex things. There are many more secondary effects. Our policymakers need to consider the risks and benefits to help us get to a better society that includes automated cars and benefits everyone.

But I'm not seeing enough discussion of one important aspect of automated cars: data, and how security, privacy and openness can increase its impact.

Automated Cars Collect a Lot of Data

As well as transporting people and parcels automated cars will collect vast amounts of data. A human driver needs to look around to see street signs, the weather or cyclists. Similarly automated cars will need to collect data to make driving decisions.

Automated cars collect a lot of data. A PhD student recently calculated that a modern car already generates 25Gb of data an hour. In

Autonomous vehicles can collect data that will inform mapping, weather, traffic reports, and directories, among other things.

2013 it was reported that Google's automated car generates 750Mb of data a second. Earlier this year Comma.ai, a company that was working on automated cars released 80Gb of data generated during $7^1/_4$ hours of driving.

This data includes such things as the car location, maps and video footage of the surrounding area, information about nearby traffic, accidents, weather information, the route of the car and information about any passengers or parcels that that are in the car.

That's a lot of data, how do we get most value from it?

Security and Privacy

The security of this data clearly needs to be considered. We need to protect the data collected by the car and the data that the car needs to be able to get to do its job. Car hacking is a real risk whilst an automated car is likely to be more dependent on access to data than a car driven by a human. Data is already an under-recognised piece of critical national infrastructure, automated cars will only increase the need to strengthen it.

Privacy will also be an important consideration. If automated cars mishandle personal data about the people travelling in them or the people and things seen by their video cameras then some people will be damaged while other people may lose trust and choose not to use the cars.

Some of these issues will be explored by smartphone apps, like Nexar, that use the smartphone's camera and microphone to collect data about car drivers, passengers, pedestrians and other cars.

But automated cars will collect far more data than a smartphone camera.

Automated Cars Will Use Data Collected by Other Cars and People

Automated car manufacturers and policymakers should be thinking about security by design, privacy by design and how openness can help build the trust that will be needed to get the most impact from automated cars. Open can help in other ways too.

The data collected by cars is needed for them to do their job but automated cars will also use data provided by other things and people.

An automated car will not wake up in a factory, blearily blink its headlights and then discover the world like a video game player constantly surprised by new things. The car will have a reasonably accurate map of the world, will get weather data (what sensible car would choose to drive into a hailstorm that might damage its paintwork?) and be able to share data with other cars.

Just as we hear of traffic jams from other people via radio alerts or smartphone apps like Waze, the people designing and building automated cars have planned for them to be able to share news about traffic congestion or improvements to their basic maps. Those improvements are vital because map data, just like any other data, is not always 100% accurate. Things change. An automated Google car driving down a street might discover that a road is blocked off, by sharing this with other Google cars it can make Google's service more efficient.

This all sounds like good use of data, but it's not good enough. We can and should do better.

Data Should Be as Open as Possible While Respecting Privacy

Sebastian Thrun of Stanford says in Werner Herzog's new documentary "Whenever a self-driving car makes a mistake, automatically all the other cars know about it, including future unborn cars." But isn't the only way that all self driving cars will "automatically" know of all other mistakes is if the data that describes those mistakes is available beyond just the automated cars of one manufacturer?

At the Open Data Institute we think that we get the most value from data when it as open as possible while respecting privacy.

The team at OpenStreetMap's 2016 April Fool's spoof was a plan to launch their own automated car. They said: "our self-driving car breaks new ground by automatically correcting OpenStreetMap data based on your driving behaviour." The story was a spoof but this bit—regardless of whether it's OpenStreetMap or another mapping organisation/community relevant to a particular country or city—is one of the ways that cars can share data with each other and with other people.

Mapping is a shared problem. All cars, automated or not, will benefit from better maps. As will pedestrians, cyclists, local authorities planning new infrastructure investments, etcetera. Collaboratively maintaining open mapping data between all of these people can reduce costs and improve quality. Facebook are happy to collaboratively maintain open mapping data as they recognise the value in this approach. Automated car manufacturers, mapping organisations and policymakers should be too.

Reducing accidents is another shared problem. The machine learning algorithms that will drive automated cars will learn faster and more accurately from more data. Sharing detailed data about the conditions in place when an accident occurred will save lives.

People will ask an automated car to drop them off at an address. That address may not be in the current list of addresses—perhaps it's a new flat?—so the person may teach the automated car where it is. The address could then be sent to an open address register as a potential improvement to the data. The next automated car will know about it but addresses are vital for many other things from pizza delivery to an ambulance. We should be maintaining addresses as efficiently and openly as possible. Collaborative maintenance helps with that and openness means that anyone can use it.

There will be many other types of data collected by the car that when opened up in this way will improve transport services, save lives and make things better in other sectors.

Live weather conditions (something that the lovely folk at TransportAPI are working on). Air quality. Congestion data. Aggregated movement of people around a city. Etcetera.

This impact of opening up this data will be felt not just in better automated car services but in other services and sectors that use the same datasets. Automated car manufacturers are in the transport business, not the mapping or air quality business. Publishing the data openly will help them tackle shared problems and increase the impact of the data. Everyone benefits from better and more open data.

Automated Car Data Should Be Secure, Private, and Open by Design

The transport sector has long been a leader in open data. The countries and organisations that have taken the lead in opening up this data have benefitted both from better services for people and through the creation of innovative new services like GoogleMaps and companies like CityMapper, Transport API and ITOWorld that create jobs and help get the data used.

As that seemingly inevitable next wave of change occurs with the rollout of automated cars that will improve transport, free up space, save lives by reducing accidents and impact jobs let's make sure we don't forget about the data infrastructure that is necessary for those cars do their job and can create so much value for the rest of our society.

Making that data infrastructure secure, private and open by design will benefit everyone.

EVALUATING THE AUTHOR'S ARGUMENTS:

In this viewpoint, Peter Wells discusses the importance of data sharing. Do you think his argument is persuasive and realistic enough to convince the automotive industry to share such data with other industries? Why or why not?

Chapter 3

Will Self-Driving Cars Become the Norm in the Next Ten Years?

Will driverless cars serve the same function as subways and other public transit?

Viewpoint

1

Self-Driving Cars Will Soon Become More Common

Philip E. Ross

"What's most striking about the new thinking is how suddenly it jelled."

In the following viewpoint, Philip E. Ross argues that science fiction of the past is quickly becoming the reality of the near future. He notes that although fully-autonomous vehicles won't fill our roads and highways in the next decade, within thirty years they will make all the driving decisions. Incrementally, they will become so "smart" that they will talk to each other, to traffic signs, and to our devices. They will solve problems of traffic jams, accidents, and parking crises. And they will bring monumental changes to the designs of our cities, our neighborhoods, and the cars themselves. Ross is a senior editor at *IEEE Spectrum*.

AS YOU READ, CONSIDER THE FOLLOWING QUESTIONS:
1. Which science fiction writer does the author use to frame the viewpoint?
2. By what year did Nissan's chief executive pledge to introduce a line of autonomous cars?
3. What are the potential benefits of sharing self-driving cars?

"Driverless Cars: Optional by 2024, Mandatory by 2044," by Philip E. Ross, *IEEE Spectrum*, May 29, 2014. Reprinted by permission.

Road design and integration could change once self-driving vehicles dominate the transportation landscape.

Sixty years ago this month, Isaac Asimov published a short story about a self-driving "automatobile" called Sally who had not only judgment but feelings, which spelled doom for the man who loved her.

It will happen—and it won't. Fully automated cars will be common. Those cars will have judgment, and this will upend our lives, our work, and our cities. But cars will have no more feeling than IBM's Deep Blue had back in 1997, when it beat the world chess champion. Well, two out of three isn't half bad, even for an Asimov.

Today you can buy a top-of-the-line S-Class car from Mercedes-Benz that figuratively says "ahem" when you begin to stray out of your lane or tailgate. If you do nothing, it'll turn the wheel slightly or lightly apply the brakes. And if you're still intent on crashing, it will take command. In 5 years, cars will be quicker to intervene; in 20, they won't need your advice; and in 30, they won't take it.

The Far-Reaching Impact

Accident rates will plummet, parking problems will vanish, streets will narrow, cities will bulk up, and commuting by automobile will become a mere extension of sleep, work, and recreation. With no steering column and no need for a crush zone in front of the passenger compartment (after all, there aren't going to be any crashes), car design will run wild: Collapsibility! Stackability! Even interchangeability, because when a car can come when called, pick up a second or third passenger for a fee, and park itself, even the need to own the thing will dwindle.

"When we modeled that for Ann Arbor, Mich., we found we'd need only 15 percent of the cars now owned there," for a per-mile cost savings of 75 percent, says Larry Burns, director of the Program on Sustainable Mobility at the Earth Institute of Columbia University, in New York City. Burns is no ivory-tower academic: In his previous job he headed up research and development for General Motors.

What's most striking about the new thinking is how suddenly it jelled. Two MIT economists, Erik Brynjolfsson and Andrew McAfee, write about the switch in their recent book, *The Second Machine Age*, in which they describe their 2012 spin in the Google self-driving car as almost "boring" because the car drove "exactly the way we're all taught to in driver's ed." They then note that the experience "was especially weird for us because only a few years earlier we were sure that computers would not be able to drive cars."

Many others were just as sure. Read what Frank Levy of MIT and Richard Murnane of Harvard wrote about the challenge of city driving back in 2004, in their book *The New Division of Labor*:

> *As the driver makes his left turn against traffic, he confronts a wall of images and sounds generated by oncoming cars, traffic lights, storefronts, billboards, trees, and a traffic policeman. Using his knowledge, he must estimate the size and position of each of these objects and the likelihood that they pose a hazard ... Articulating this knowledge and embedding it in software for all but highly structured situations are at present enormously difficult tasks.*

A year after those lines were written, Sebastian Thrun led the Stanford team's car to victory in the DARPA Grand Challenge, the Defense Advanced Research Projects Agency's autonomous vehicle race. Two years later, Google hired Thrun. And in 2010 Thrun's group unveiled Google's car.

Current Developments

Why the sudden change? Maybe it had to do with the ongoing drop in the cost of radar, infrared imagers, sonar, GPS, and other sensors. Or maybe it was the dramatic improvement in the processing power of embedded systems. Or it could be that engineers had just gotten comfortable with such building-block technologies as adaptive cruise control, automatic parking, and navigation.

In any case, by the beginning of this decade every major automaker was working on autonomous driving. The most in-your-face firm, as usual, is Nissan Motor Co., whose chief executive, Carlos Ghosn, recently promised to introduce not one car but a line of cars that can drive themselves—by 2020. Big talk, you may say, but in 2007 Ghosn vowed to deliver the all-electric Leaf by 2010, and he did.

Interesting, also, is Volvo's growing investment in autonomous driving technology. As part of the European research project known as SARTRE (Social Attitudes to Road Traffic Risk in Europe), the final version of which ran from 2009 to 2012, Volvo supplied cars that automatically followed in a line behind a truck driven by a professional driver, saving effort and fuel.

A lead engineer in that project, Erik Coelingh, says Volvo is using a fleet of 100 cars to test out autonomy in the Swedish city of Gothenburg. Such validation will take time, he adds, no matter how fast other technologies may advance. "Even if you've tested the system in 10 cars and it works fine, with not a single incident, it doesn't tell you a lot about how 100 000 cars will do on the road."

He sees the technology advancing by degrees, beginning in test-bed cities like Gothenburg and in places where pedestrians aren't allowed—say, within mines in Australia, where huge robotrucks are already carrying ore. Next come traffic jams, where movement is slow and there is no oncoming traffic. Then, he says, come selected routes, every meter of which has been carefully validated, so that a driver can just "punch a button to drive autonomously."

Testing will proceed road by road and city by city, Coelingh says, building to the point at which cars can plan the route and take you there, from door to door. But he figures it'll be 10 years for the first commercial robocars (that's three more years than Ghosn predicts), and 20 before they take up a big share of new sales. However, he allows, autonomy could come faster in places where much of the infrastructure is only now being put in, like China. (By the way, Volvo is now owned by Geely Automobile, a Chinese firm.)

Changes to Infrastructure

Where infrastructure is designed with robocars in mind, many of the hardest problems will be easy to solve. Cars will talk to the road, to the traffic signs, and to one another. What one car up ahead can see, all will know about. Even the problem of identifying pedestrians lurking behind shrubbery will finally fade away: After all, if cars can talk to signs, they can certainly talk to the cellphone in your pocket. Traffic accidents will be rare enough to be as shocking as they should be.

Asimov wrote not of robocars but of their consequences. He thus followed the sci-fi rule of his colleague, Frederik Pohl, "to predict not the automobile but the traffic jam."

In that spirit, let's assume that fully autonomous vehicles mature without worrying too much about the technology needed. What would happen? Briefly, our roads, our towns, and the frames of our lives will change, as they did when cars were first introduced.

"Approximately every two generations, we rebuild the transportation infrastructure in our cities in ways that shape the vitality of neighborhoods; the settlement patterns in our cities and countryside; and our economy, society, and culture," writes Marlon G. Boarnet, a specialist in transportation and urban growth at the University of Southern California.

Robocars would be shared, and that would make them both convenient and cheap to use. Vehicles would be fewer in number but far more heavily used, picking up new passengers near where they left the last ones off. Such vehicle-sharing schemes are spreading, even though today's dumb vehicles tend not to be there for you when you need them. One reason is that they accumulate at popular destinations. It'd be different for a car that could come when you called and leave when you were done with it.

"Certainly, car sharing is an option," says Ralf Herrtwich, a leader in Mercedes's autonomous car project, in Stuttgart. "Get the vehicle at your command, drop it at your convenience, no parking."

Brave talk, but Mercedes owners must quail at the thought of a commodified sharemobile. Who would pay a higher fare for a robotaxi lined in burled walnut, with leather seats and a perfume dispenser—features actually offered in the 2014 Mercedes S-Class?

There's one bunch who won't be able to pay for such fripperies: professional drivers. Say good-bye to all of them—5 million people in the United States alone. In a world of autonomous cargo carriage, machines could hitch trucks to standardized containers of stuff. Then, at distribution points, other machines could transfer their contents to smaller trucks—or perhaps to robots so small they could safely roll along sidewalks. Picture a little triwheeler that would fail only by stopping, not by falling on your head, as one of Amazon.com's proposed quadcopter delivery drones might do.

"Could we enter into a world where things are brought to us in a Segway-size pod?" wonders Burns of Columbia. "And if so, what does that do to retail big-box stores?"

Say bye-bye as well to the soccer mom. Parents will call a robocab, set its parental controls, lock the car doors, and send their teenage daughters to practice or maybe to the library, making it impossible for them to cruise "through the hamburger stand now," as the Beach Boys sang in 1964.

The self-driving car will free us of much drudgery, true, but future generations may never know the freedom of the open road. And though the work such a car will do will be of great value, it probably won't inspire many songs.

EVALUATING THE AUTHOR'S ARGUMENTS:

In this viewpoint, Philip E. Ross illustrates a changing American landscape resulting from self-driving cars. How do you think the rollout of autonomous vehicles will change your own neighborhood and your life?

Fully Autonomous Cars Are a Long Way Off

> *"Driving a partially automated vehicle may be harder than driving a vehicle today."*

Jarrett Walker

In the following viewpoint, Jarrett Walker argues that the arrival of fully autonomous cars is a long way off, if indeed even possible at all. Walker maintains that although some driverless models at a level 2 technology are in production, it will be difficult to achieve the next three levels of driverless technology up to level 5, or a fully automated car able to drive door-to-door. Walker is an international consultant writing about issues of public transit and transportation design, including the book *Human Transit: How Clearer Thinking About Public Transit Can Enrich Our Communities and Our Lives.*

AS YOU READ, CONSIDER THE FOLLOWING QUESTIONS:

1. According to the viewpoint's table, what level of automation exists, and what level designates a fully automated vehicle?
2. What is the biggest difficulty of level 3 automation as reported by Walker?
3. Why is automated transit easier, according to the author?

"Are Fully Driverless Vehicles Coming Soon? Doubts, and Smarter Hopes," Human Transit, October 26, 2016. Reprinted by permission.

Will car salespeople have fewer cars to sell when—and if—fully automated vehicles take off?

The endless debate about how fully automated cars would change our cities often starts with the assumption that we will have fully automated cars soon. We imagine that we'll all be riding around in totally automated taxis, whose lack of a driver will make them cheap.

This is the essence of the "driverless cars will replace transit" fantasy. I've argued many times that this idea is geometrically incoherent in dense cities, because regardless of automation there isn't enough room to move people from big transit vehicles into small ones.

But it's also important to ask: *How soon is this truly driverless vehicle really coming?*

Levels of Automation

Here is the standard 1–5 scale, by SAE International, that everybody uses to talk about this. Level 1 technology is available now, but the kind of automation that totally eliminates a driver, thus transforming the economics of all hired transportation, comes only at Level 5.

Title: Levels of Automation

Automation Level	Driver's Role	Technology	Status
0	Driver operates vehicle		Available now
1	Driver holds wheel or controls pedals	Vehicle steers or controls speed	Available now
2	Driver monitors at all times	Vehicle drives itself—not 100% safely	Vehicles in production
3	Driver ready to regain control	Vehicle drives itself—but may give up control	Not available
4	Driver not required at all times	Vehicle drives itself during specific use case, such as the highway	Not available
5	Driver not needed; fully automated	Vehicle drives itself door to door	Far in the future

FAST FACT

In January 2017, the first autonomous electric bus ran for a ten-day trial in Las Vegas, Nevada.

Most experts seem to agree we will soon have Level 2, enhanced driver-assistance that shifts the driver to more of a monitoring role, but that the journey to Level 5, actually eliminating the driver, is a long one that has only begun.

Steven E Shladover, from the PATH program at UC Berkeley, has been thinking about vehicle technology for decades. In his excellent (and tragically paywalled) piece for *Scientific American* this June, he noted some of the reasons why full automation is so hard, and requires solving problems that are not just technological.

A fully automated vehicle needs to be able to do the right thing [in] *any* situation, and handle its own equipment failures. In big airplanes, this is achieved only through multiple redundant systems that make the product massively expensive. Nobody knows how to scale an airliner's level of redundancy to an affordable mass-market vehicle.

Crossing the Ravine of Distraction at Level 3

The biggest barrier to full Level 5 automation may also be a reason to leap to it prematurely. It's human reaction time at the *intermediate* levels of automation. Shladover:

> *The prospects for level three automation are clouded, too, because of the very real problem of recapturing the attention, in an emergency, of a driver who has zoned out while watching the scenery go by or, worse, who has fallen asleep. I have heard representatives from some automakers say that this is such a hard problem that they simply will not attempt level three. Outside of traffic jam assistants that take over in stop and go traffic, where speeds are so low that a worst case collision would be a fender bender,* **it is conceivable that level three automation will never happen**. *[Emphasis added.]*

Anyone examining their own experience will see that this is a big problem, and that it's not a technological problem.

To make this more vivid, let's stop and think what the opposite of automation is. It's an old mid-century car, maybe my parents' 1962 International Scout, a tough precursor to today's SUVs. The primitive suspension pounded your body with the textures of the road. Your hand on the stick-shift felt the movement of the gears. When something shoved back against your attempt to turn, the steering wheel sent the shove right up your arms. To stop fast, you had to pound the brakes with your weight. Nothing pretended to protect you from the weather. With all this vivid input flowing into you, demanding constant decisions, you would never fall asleep at the wheel, or be tempted to look at the newspaper on your seat. Driving was hard, but often ecstatic. When power steering and automatic transmissions came along, my elders agreed that by reducing the level of effort and stimulation, these inventions made driving harder to focus on.

The journey from here to Level 3 looks just like the journey from the Scout to here. It's the same straight-line path from vividness toward tedium, from control to passivity. It ends at a faintly ridiculous extreme: you sit there, unstimulated and with nothing to do, but you must still pay attention. We could reach a point where the only safe "drivers" are people with years of meditation training, since nothing else prepares you for that situation. And all that training would be expensive, pushing drivers' wages up!

At Level 3, Forward or Back?

If the Level 3 problem is as hard as it looks, how will we respond? Tech-optimists will see this as a reason to rush even faster to Level 5, maybe prematurely. But many people who get a taste of Level 3 will be keen to stop at Level 2, where they still feel like they're in control. Level 3 accidents, caused by human inattention but easily blamed on the technology, would inflame both sides in this debate.

At that point, will the reason to go forward be safety? We don't know, because we don't know what the impact of Level 2 will be on fatality rates. Maybe they will have improved so drastically that Level

5 doesn't offer that much more, or at least not enough more to make the public ready to accept the loss of control at that level.

So the other issue will be the liberation of labor, especially professional drivers. All the dreams of driverless taxis, for example, require getting all the way to Level 5. Maybe it will happen, starting with fleets, but the question of whether you can jump over the ravine of distraction at Level 3, and land all the way at Level 5, is an open one.

Are we sure driverless vehicles will be cheap and abundant soon? I have no idea, and nobody else does either, but the path does not look easy.

Automated Transit Is Easier!

So what does this all mean for transit? You read it here first: Full automation of transit is much easier than automation of cars. (If it's impossible, that's only because driverless cars turn out to be impossible.) Shladover:

> *And yet we will see highly automated cars [vehicles?] soon, probably within the coming decade. Nearly every big automaker and many information technology companies are devoting serious resources to level four automation: fully automated driving,* **restricted to specific environments***, that does not rely on a fallible human for backup.* **When you limit the situations in which automated vehicle systems must operate, you greatly increase their feasibility.** *[Emphasis added.]*

High-ridership fixed route transit vehicles are perfect examples of this possibility. They run on pre-set paths in a narrow range of situations. In fact, the busier they are, the more money we should spend to make these situations narrower: exclusive lanes, automated stopping and fare collection, weather protection technologies, and potentially limits on lateral motion, up to and including rail. Unlike vehicles that could go anywhere, automated transit vehicles don't need a map of absolutely everywhere. All of these things make transit automation easier. In effect, transit is a case where you can get full automation with Level 4 technology.

I am not making light of the considerable challenge of managing the impact of the transformation of the workforce wrought by automation. I am very concerned about those impacts. But the effect of automation on work is an issue in many fields, and when it becomes critical we will find a collective solution. Smart people are thinking about it.

Takeaways:

- Full automation of any kind, going anywhere, the goal that replaces most human labor, is quite a ways off and requires overcoming several obstacles that nobody has cracked yet. It may not be possible.
- Driving a partially automated vehicle may be harder than driving a vehicle today, because the distraction problem gets worse. This may increase the skill level of the labor required, and thus the labor cost.
- But the distraction problem with partial automation may also cause a premature rush to full automation, plus a strong movement to stop at Level 2.
- Technologically and spatially, high-ridership fixed-route transit is much more easily automated than any other vehicle under discussion today, because it operates in such limited situations. Fully automated rail transit, in regular service, is over 30 years old. Driverless buses are under development and present especially promising options especially in fixed rights of way.
- If driverless transit were ever achieved, the explosive growth in transit abundance would be extraordinary, because labor cost is the main limiting factor today. This vast increase [in] transit would mean cities could grow denser with less traffic, putting more opportunities within a shorter travel time for everyone.
- But again, full automation may not be possible. We don't know.

I am not sure what we will do about this, apart from telling the "we-should-neglect-transit-because-driverless-cars" people to take a cold shower. But that's the terrain ahead, and to me, it looks like transit has a very promising future.

EVALUATING THE AUTHOR'S ARGUMENTS:

In this viewpoint, Jarrett Walker argues that it will be many years, if ever, before a fully autonomous car will be ready for drivers. Walker argues that instead, the technology should be focused on driverless transit. Do you agree with Walker? Present your case either for or against focusing on driverless transit, using evidence from the viewpoint.

Viewpoint 3

Will Autonomous Cars Result in Utopia or Dystopia?

Phil McKenna

"The pace at which autonomous cars are coming on is dramatically faster than what people had imagined."

In the following viewpoint, Phil McKenna debates whether self-driving car technology will result in a utopian or dystopian culture. According to studies cited by McKenna, much depends on geographical location, the mind-set of drivers, and the cost of technology, which affects the price of transportation. McKenna also points out that transportation users will either embrace or disregard ride sharing, and this factor will impact the future. McKenna is a staff writer for InsideClimate News and likes to focus on individuals making news in energy and the environment.

AS YOU READ, CONSIDER THE FOLLOWING QUESTIONS:

1. Identify the assumption made by think tanks that paint a positive picture about the future of self-driving cars, as stated in the viewpoint.
2. How does Marchetti's constant apply to self-driving technology?
3. According to the author, what technologies have made sharing of self-driving cars possible?

"Urban Transit's Uncertain Future," by Phil McKenna, WGBH Educational Foundation, January 13, 2016. Reprinted by permission.

A lot of challenges need to be solved before we can expect a fully driverless world.

Imagine if nine out of every ten cars suddenly disappeared from city streets. On-street parking would be eliminated entirely, giving way to restaurant seating, bike paths, and green space. Parking garages would all but disappear, making room for additional housing, retail, and office space.

Now imagine if cities around the world sprawled for hundreds of miles, their centers clogged with twice today's car traffic, and daily commutes lasted for hours. Both scenarios, it turns out, are entirely plausible futures with the rise of autonomous vehicles, the self-driving cars now navigating city streets from Silicon Valley to Singapore.

"There is a huge potential for change," says Philippe Crist, an economist with the Organization for Economic Co-operation and Development (OECD). "It creates new possibilities that we are only starting to get our minds around." The OECD is one of a growing number of think tanks and institutions peering into the crystal ball of urban mobility's future and, more often than not, conjuring rosy expectations. Fleets of shared, self-driving vehicles could indeed remove nine out of every ten vehicles on city streets, eliminating the need for all on-street parking and 80% of off-street parking, according to a recent study by the group.

The Paris-based think tank's assessment comes from simulations of Lisbon, Portugal, a mid-sized European city, based on real trip-taking activity and assuming that people rode in self-driving cars that can be shared simultaneously by several passengers. The findings were comparable to similar recent studies of shared autonomous vehicles in New York, New Jersey, Ann Arbor, Michigan, and Singapore.

The significant reduction in vehicles—a 90% drop in cars over a 24-hour period and 70% fewer vehicles during peak travel periods—comes through sharing of cars that today typically sit unused 23 hours per day. "The arrival of this technology allows consumers, or companies, to extract value from these stranded assets the rest of the day," Crist says.

While autonomous vehicles may sound futuristic, self-driving cars are increasingly part of the present. Last January, Mercedes-Benz introduced the F 015 Luxury in Motion self-driving concept car with front seats that can swivel away from the windshield to face the rear seats. In March, industry supplier Delphi Automotive drove from San Francisco to New York in an Audi Q5 piloted almost entirely by radar, cameras, and laser sensors. And Google, which has already logged over 1.3 million driving miles with autonomous vehicles, is now building a fleet of 100 next-generation prototypes. In June, the vehicles, each of which looks like a large computer mouse, began navigating city streets from Silicon Valley to San Francisco.

"The pace at which autonomous cars are coming on is dramatically faster than what people had imagined," says Robin Chase, former CEO of car sharing company Zipcar.

Utopia or Something Else?

While autonomous vehicles are coming, it's still entirely unclear what their arrival will bring. If everyone rides in an autonomous vehicle, there will be few if any accidents, which will allow for lighter, more fuel-efficient vehicles. And if people share these vehicles as they move about the city, the total miles driven each day will also decrease. Combine lighter cars with fewer miles traveled, and the amount of energy used to get people where they need to go drops by 80%. This, at least, is the "utopian scenario" in a recent study by researchers at Lawrence Berkeley National Laboratory.

Yet in the study's "dystopian scenario," energy consumption more than doubles as larger, privately owned vehicles travel longer distances. "You could imagine a consumer wanting to be able to cook dinner on their way home or to watch movies while the car is driving, and they could then not care if they lived close to their work place," says lead author William Morrow.

Luís Bettencourt, a professor of complex systems at the Santa Fe Institute in New Mexico, who was not involved with the study, thinks a dystopian outcome is more likely. "I think the expectation is they would tend to make cities bigger and less dense," he says. Bettencourt, whose research focuses on cities and urbanization, cites Marchetti's constant. Named for the Venetian physicist who devised it, Marchetti's constant states that throughout history, no matter where people lived or what form of transportation they used to get about, they have always spent and will continue to spend an average of 30 minutes each way getting to and from work. Autonomous vehicles could speed up commutes, allowing people to live farther apart, Bettencourt says.

"Once you have autonomous vehicles and algorithmic ways of coordinating traffic, then the obvious next step is you start coordinating vehicles into convoys. You can imagine 200 mph corridors where these trains made out of cars are just moving across the city, and those would be the future highways."

Bettencourt questions why the reduction in vehicles, predicted by many, hasn't already occurred. "We've had taxi services for a while, and we have Uber and new incarnations of those same services," he says. "Why aren't these things taking over cities entirely? Why do we still insist on buying a car?"

Fewer people, however, are insisting on buying cars. Recent studies suggest car ownership in the US peaked during the last decade and is now on the decline. One study conducted by researchers at the University of Michigan's Transportation Research Institute in Ann Arbor found more than 30% of households do not own a car in six out of 30 of the largest US cities. In New York City, 57% of households do not have a vehicle, up from 54% in 2007.

A separate study by the same institute found a significant decrease in recent years in the number of young drivers across 15 countries. The decrease correlated strongly with internet access, suggesting that virtual contact via electronic devices may be reducing the need for actual contact.

FAST FACT

Ninety-five percent of passenger miles traveled in the United States could be in autonomous electric cars owned by on-demand transportation companies by the year 2030.

Rise of the Taxibot

Electronic devices may not only be reducing interest in car ownership but are enabling the sharing of vehicles that make shared, self-driving vehicles possible.

"You couldn't have imagined this ten years ago when people didn't have smart phones and mobile computing was not available," says Emilio Frazzoli, head of Future Urban Mobility for the Singapore-MIT Alliance for Research and Technology. "Now you have this ability to connect and book a car. You see it with Uber and the proliferation of taxi booking apps or public transportation schedule routing apps, and this is at the same time you have autonomous vehicle technology that is evolving. You can marry the two."

Sharing of non-autonomous vehicles already offers a distinct advantage over traditional car ownership, says Chase, author of the book *Peers Inc* and a champion of the sharing economy. "If you are financially smart and you are living in the city and you don't need a car to get to work, you are insane to own one," she says. "You will always be saving money by renting them when you need them."

Further savings come when people not only share a car but also share the ride. Ride-sharing startups Uber and Lyft now offer UberPool and Lyft Line, carpooling services that allow people headed in the same direction to share a ride. "In San Francisco today, UberPool is $7 to go from anywhere to anywhere. That's probably one-third the cost of a taxi," says Xavier Mosquet, a senior partner at the Boston Consulting Group.

If a private company could use an autonomous vehicle rather than paying a driver, the cost of transporting people across the city would be even less. A recent study by the Boston Consulting Group found the cost of conveying one passenger by an autonomous vehicle would be 35% less than by conventional taxi at the average taxi occupancy rate of 1.2 passengers. Increase an autonomous vehicle's rate of occupancy to just two passengers and the cost per passenger becomes competitive with mass transit.

Mosquet says such shared, autonomous vehicles may not work everywhere but will be well suited for the world's 50 to 100 largest cities where population density is greatest. "In Manhattan, you have ten people looking for the same cab and mostly likely headed in the same direction on every corner," he says. "With a smartphone now collecting that information, using it is extremely easy."

Where demand is high, larger, driverless buses could give autonomous vehicles an added advantage. Today, the Exclusive Bus Lane (XBL), a 2.5 mile stretch of highway connecting the New Jersey Turnpike with midtown Manhattan, is the busiest bus lane in America, with the capacity to transport up to 41,000 people per hour through the Lincoln Tunnel. Self-driving buses could reduce the time between vehicles from five seconds to one second, allowing the tunnel to accommodate more than 200,000 passengers per hour, according to a recent study by researchers at Princeton University.

Singapore and a number of European countries are now testing or preparing to test fully autonomous buses that could complement fleets of self-driving cars. "You can combine different types of transportation to provide both the convenience that people need with the scalability that a city needs," Frazzoli says.

Detours Ahead

Before fleets of self-driving cars or buses can replace the cars of today, a number of challenges still need to be addressed. Among a range of sensor technologies for autonomous vehicles that includes radar, ultrasound, and cameras, laser-based "LiDAR" sensors shows the most promise. The technology, however, has been incredibly expensive. The LiDAR sensors that Google used on its first generation prototype cost $80,000 per vehicle and $8,000 per vehicle for its current prototype, Mosquet says. Costs continue to drop quickly. Just last week, automotive startup Quanergy announced a solid-state LiDAR system that will cost under $250 when it enters mass production later this year.

Apart from technical issues, a significant challenge may simply be gaining widespread adoption. The best case scenario of the recent OECD study—where shared autonomous cars take nine out of ten vehicles off city streets—is based on the assumption that everyone rides in an autonomous vehicle and shares each trip with others headed in the same direction. If half of a city's population continues to drive their own cars, the number of vehicles—and the amount of time people spend idling in traffic jams—could actually increase.

EVALUATING THE AUTHOR'S ARGUMENTS:

In this viewpoint, Phil McKenna debates whether the arrival and widespread usage of autonomous cars will cause a utopian or dystopian culture. How do you see this situation? Does living in a big city and forgoing car ownership make sense? Why? Does living in a suburban or rural area and owning a car make sense? Why?

Viewpoint 4

Nontechnical Challenges Could Prevent Self-Driving Cars from Taking Off

Jon Walker

"When we get self-driving cars 'depends more on political factors than on technological factors.'"

In the following viewpoint, Jon Walker debates the issues concerning how self-driving cars may or may not become common on the roads. Walker argues that two types of challenges—human behavior and legal—will likely hold back this technology for some time to come. Another interesting twist that Walker argues is the angle of interference by lobbyists representing workers who would likely lose their jobs because of automation. Walker reports on issues concerning industry and artificial intelligence.

AS YOU READ, CONSIDER THE FOLLOWING QUESTIONS:

1. What most likely caused the crash of Tesla's self-driving car?
2. Identify one obstacle to self-driving cars caused by regulations and laws as reported by the author.
3. How could lobbyists hold back development of self-driving cars?

"Autonomous Vehicle Regulations—Near-Term Challenges and Consequences," by Jon Walker, TechEmergence, September 7, 2017. Reprinted by permission.

Whether a lot full of autonomous vehicles becomes a common sight depends on several factors, and not all of them have to do with technology.

Several car makers predict they will able to make true self-driving cars in the next few years—as we've covered in our recent self-driving car timeline article. This technology, though, is only valuable if there are plenty of roads these self-driving cars are legally allowed to travel on. Even if the technologies allow for true autonomy, without legal permission the self-driving cars are mostly worthless to individuals and companies.

Even if the industry does manage to overcome the numerous technical challenges required to make cars capable of safely driving themselves (which remains a real technical challenge), that doesn't assure that the technology will see massive deployment once they do. The industry will also need to deal with legal, behavioral, and economic challenges before we reach a point where self-driving cars can be ubiquitous.

This article examines several of the biggest non-technical challenges self-driving cars could face and how the industry hopes to overcome these issues. Most of these hurdles are intertwined in complex ways, but for simplicity this article will break down the challenges into two main categories:

- The human behavior challenges, which include how people often misuse technology or are scared by change.
- The legal challenges, which include issues like regulatory restrictions, political blowback, and special interest lobbying concerns.

When we get self-driving cars "depends more on political factors than on technological factors" Hod Lipson, Professor of Engineering at Columbia University, and co-author of *Driverless: Intelligent Cars and the Road Ahead* told TechEmergence. Lipson says the technology is getting better at an exponential, "But law and policy isn't keeping pace … Until governments sets a clear and simple goal, companies don't know what to aim for and consumer don't know what to expect."

To understand the non-technical hurdles autonomous vehicles will face first requires an understanding of how the technology will be used and categorized.

What Self-Driving Even Means

The Society of Automotive Engineers defines a vehicle's autonomous capacity on a scale of 0–5. They are effectively:

- Level 0—No Automation
- Level 1—Driver Assistance—Basic driver assistance like automatic braking.
- Level 2—Partial Automation—Advanced driver assistance like cruise control combined with automatic lane centering, but the human driver needs to monitor conditions at all times.
- Level 3—Conditional Automation—Under specific conditions the car can drive itself, but a human driver needs to be ready to quickly respond to a request to intervene.
- Level 4—High Automation—The vehicle is capable of safely driving itself without ever needing to request a human to intervene, but it can only drive itself under specific conditions/pre-mapped territories (such as a mapped downtown area).
- Level 5—Full Automation—The vehicle can drive itself anywhere under any conditions.

The technical challenges involved in creating a car that can drive itself in every conceivable environment and under every condition means we will not likely see true Level 5 autonomy for a while. For example, Volvo's autonomous car AI has more difficulty predicting the hopping movement of kangaroos than the running movement of most other mammals—a problem they have spent years trying to solve.

Instead, Level 2, Level 3, and Level 4 autonomy are what we are currently seeing and are likely to see in the near future. The problem is that anytime that you include humans in the process, you create room for human error. There are several ways this human involvement can created unique technical and legal problems.

Autonomous Vehicle Regulations—
Issues of Human Behavior
The Hand-Off Problem

In theory, a car with a Level 2 or Level 3 system that can automatically perform 90 percent of all important driving tasks and automatically avoid most accidents would be much safer than a car without one, but in practice it doesn't exactly work this way.

Humans are easily distracted, and it takes them several seconds to mentally switch from one task to another, which could mean life or death when driving at 70 mph. Unless a person is constantly involved in the driving process, it is easy for them to become, bored, highly distracted or even fall asleep.

A system that is good enough but not yet perfect can lull individuals into a false sense of security, resulting in a catastrophic failure. This means Level 2 and Level 3 systems require a way to keep drivers alert and readily engaged when they have nothing to do, which in practice is no easy task. Ford tried everything including lights, loud noises, vibrations, and even a copilot to keep their engineers engaged during testing, and none of it worked.

A real life example of a driver being lulled into a false sense of security may have occurred on May 7, 2016 in a fatal crash involving a Tesla Model S. The National Highway Traffic Safety Administration (NHTSA) investigation found that the car was in Autopilot mode (Level 2 technology) when it collided with a tractor trailer.

Even though the trailer "should have been visible to the Tesla driver for at least seven seconds prior to impact," the driver took no action to avoid it. This likely indicates the driver was not paying attention, despite Tesla's explicit warnings to drivers about the limitations of their Autopilot system and their use of built-in systems to keep drivers alert.

This hand-off issue is so bad companies like Ford, Volvo, and Waymo have decided to effectively avoid Level 3 cars all together. Even the car companies that are pursuing Level 3 are dramatically limiting their use. For example, Audi claims their new Traffic Jam Pilot is Level 3, but drivers can only use it when stuck in very slow traffic on limited-access, divided highways.

Liability

This hand-off problem also raises a legal liability issue. If an accident is caused by a car with zero automation, the driver is obviously to blame. Similarly, if a vehicle completely under AI control causes an accident, the liability would fall on the car marker/software provider. Google (now Waymo), Mercedes, and Volvo have said they would accept liability for their autonomous systems.

Who exactly is liable, though if a Level 2 or Level 3 vehicle gets in an accident? If the car warns a driver but the driver doesn't react in time, is the car or the driver at fault? What is an appropriate amount of time and level of warning before a hand off? We might imagine that this kind of an issue would be even more concerning with larger, heavier self-driving trucks.

These are questions without an easy answer or even one answer. Liability laws and legal precedent vary significantly from country to country and even from state to state. Without national regulation, there are no real guidelines for how possible cases might be decided. Moreover, given the technology is so new, there are few existing lawsuits to look at.

Common law is based on judicial precedent. Decisions by high courts on new legal issues effectively bind lower courts and give anyone an expectation of how laws will be enforced. Until a body of cases involve these technology work their way through the courts it is unknown how the judiciary will treat these liability issues.

Fearing What's New and Unknown

In general, people have an irrational fear of new dangers and become too complacent about established dangers. This can be a problem for self-driving cars.

Take, for example, this fatal Tesla crash in Florida. It was covered by a number of media outlets including the *New York Times*, the *Guardian*, Reuters, and the *Washington Post*.

Now consider that, according to the NHTSA, just over 35,000 people died in roadway crashes in 2015. That means on May 7, 2016, when Joshua Brown was killed in the Tesla accident, roughly 100 other people likely died in regular car accidents. None of these other normal traffic deaths generated anywhere near the level of national and international press since they weren't unexpected or new.

This disproportionate media focus on any death involving an autonomous car will likely continue, and there will be more deaths. According to the NHTSA, 94 percent of accidents are caused by human error—so while theoretically perfect self-driving cars can eliminate most accidents, even they won't stop all of them. While rare, there are always going to be problems (like freak rock slides, or deer jumping into the road) that probably can't be avoided.

Heavy media attention around autonomous vehicle accidents and irrational fear can make individuals more scared of something new than they should be based on the statistics. This can create a political environment that is more difficult for new regulation.

Autonomous Vehicle Regulations— the Legal Challenges

The legal hurdles that might slow the deployment of autonomous cars are numerous but can be divided into two areas. On one hand, bureaucracy often moves slower than technology changes. On the other hand is the political considerations.

Even if an administration nominally supports the technology, public agencies are required to be diligent in writing new regulations. Additionally, legislators often have more pressing issues to take up than bills about a technology that may or may not actually exist in the future.

Regulatory Patchwork

The United States' federal agencies are, at the moment, very supportive of self-driving car technology, but they admit they currently don't have the regulatory structure or statutory authority necessary to make it work. In self-driving car guidelines issued last year, the Department of Transportation wrote:

> The more effective use of NHTSA's existing regulatory tools will help to expedite the safe introduction and regulation of new HAVs [highly automated vehicles]. However, because today's governing statutes and regulations were developed when HAVs were only a remote notion, those tools may not be sufficient to ensure that HAVs are introduced safely, and to realize the full safety promise of new technologies.

The paper highlights several places where the Department of Transportation would potentially need new legislation such as pre-market approval and cease-and-desist powers.

While the department continues to let states experiment with self-driving car regulations as they work on their own rules, they acknowledge it is not a good long-term solution. The department points out the goal must be for manufacturers to be able to focus on one standard instead of "50 different versions to meet individual state requirements."

Congress has begun work on a bipartisan effort to fix this patchwork problem by giving the department the authority it needs to set national rules that pre-empt current state laws. There is no guarantee when or if Congress will get to it, given their busy legislative calendar full of more pressing issues. The industry has been wise to aggressively push for these regulatory changes well in advance of when they expect to make use of them.

Until federal action is taken, the growing patchwork of state laws will remain a mess. Currently, 20 states have adopted their own autonomous vehicle laws, and three states have executive orders on the subject. While these varying state laws have been useful for helping companies' testing, they could hinder actual commercial deployment.

Political Problems

American regulators and legislators are fairly pro-autonomous vehicles at the moment, but political opposition could emerge to actively slow or stop the process. Lobbying groups, such as taxi drivers or airlines, might oppose the technology as a direct competitor. Similarly, landowners and businesses in certain areas may be legitimately concerned about how changing commuting patterns would impact their land value.

There are roughly 1.8 million heavy truck drivers, 1.3 million delivery truck drivers, 660,000 bus drivers and 230,000 taxi drivers/chauffeurs in this country. That is a lot of people who could lose their jobs due to the technology and create a political backlash.

India's highways minister Nitin Gadkari recently claimed India won't allow self driving cars because, "We won't allow any technology that takes away jobs." He might not be the only politician to take that position once the technology starts being used.

Even the United States is no stranger to laws that prevent automation from eliminating totally unnecessary jobs. To protect jobs, Oregon and New Jersey still don't allow individuals to pump their own gas.

"It is going to be very ugly," Vivek Wadhwa distinguished fellow at Carnegie Mellon University and author of *The Driver in the Driverless Car: How Our Technology Choices Will Create the Future* told Techemergence. With so many jobs at stake and so many big changes likely to result for self-driving cars, "there are going to be [regulatory] battles everywhere." Both at the national level worldwide and big fights state by state. While Wadhwa believes "technology will win out in the end," these fights could slow the roll out of technology in many places.

It is worth noting that the first country to really let a company experiment with self-driving taxis on their roads was Singapore, a city-state which aggressively discourages car ownership and driving

—making it a country were the possible political impact of autonomous vehicles is likely to be very limited.

Beyond employment concerns, people might irrationally fear the technology is unsafe, be upset that it gives rich people some advantage, believe that "zombie cars" will cause traffic downtown, dislike them for aesthetic reasons, or just hate change.

Polling by AAA found 54 percent say they would feel less safe sharing the road with autonomous cars, and 78 percent would be afraid to ride in one. These are fears any organization which would financially be hard [hit] by the widespread use of the technology could exploit to slow it down or stop it.

Intel, which is a major producer of self-driving car components, understand this is [a] potential consumer and political problem. It has been doing extensive focus group research on the ways to best make people comfortable with the technology.

While most people probably think of telephones as a great technological advancement, back in the 1880's many groups actively fought against putting in telephone lines as blight. In some cities police cut down poles and people threatened to tar and feather workers installing them. The opposition was short lived but intense. Researchers found that it would be easy for disgruntled individuals to mess with current self-driving car AI. A simple graffiti can making traffic signs unrecognizable [to] their vision systems.

Conclusion

The way car makers and technology companies have been aggressively investing in autonomous vehicles leaves the strong impression they expect Level 4 self-driving cars to be a rapidly adopted and transformative technology. Theoretically, big improvements in safety, convenience, and efficiency would on net make society better off, so the technology should be appealing.

However, self-driving cars will only see massive deployment in countries where the government allows them on the roads. In a democracy, getting that approval requires the right political environment. For example countries where fewer people hold driving based occupations might be more politically receptive to the technology.

The issue is that at least in the beginning, the benefits for most people would likely seem modest and nebulous. At the same time, for the millions at risk of losing their jobs, the downside would likely feel huge and immediate. Even when the side that benefits vastly outnumbers the side that is losing, losers can have a disproportionate impact on policy when they are more motivated.

For example, in the United States the penny has so little value it costs the taxpayers more to make one than they one is worth. Pennies are a net drain on the government. Yet since the benefits of getting rid of [them] are rather diffuse, zinc companies have effectively lobbied for years to continue their production. Zinc is the main component of pennies.

Exploiting the public's current fear and skepticism, lobbying groups that might lose out from autonomous vehicles could generate some real traction if the technology ever starts making a real impact.

For now the economic impact debate is mostly theoretical, so it is smart that the potential autonomous car markers are pushing for the legislative and regulatory changes they need while the issue is mostly ignored. At the moment, is it going rather smoothly but that could change when the autonomous rubber meets the road and people start losing their jobs.

EVALUATING THE AUTHOR'S ARGUMENTS:

In this viewpoint, Jon Walker analyzes the effects of three types of difficulties—legal, behavioral, and political—that could potentially put the brakes on driverless technology. Where do you stand? Prepare an argument by using evidence from the viewpoint and challenge two of these three potential difficulties.

Facts About Self-Driving Cars

Editor's note: These facts can be used in reports to add credibility when making important points or claims.

Important Dates on the Road to Self-Driving Cars

- 1925: Houdina Radio Control demonstrates a radio-controlled driverless car.
- 1958: Cruise control is introduced in the Chrysler Imperial.
- 1964: Science fiction writer Isaac Asimov predicts vehicles with robot brains.
- 2003: A few cars begin to have self-parking systems.
- 2004: A contest is founded by DARPA to spur autonomous vehicle development.
- 2005: Stanford University's robot car wins the DARPA prize.
- 2009: Google begins its self-driving car project.
- 2013–2014: Many major auto companies are working on their own autonomous technologies.
- 2014: Google makes a car with no brakes, no steering wheel, and no gas pedal. It has a button to turn it on.
- 2015: Tesla sends out its special Autopilot software.
- 2016: Two accidents with self-driving cars occur.

Five Levels of Car Automation Explained

- Level 0: There is no automation. The driver controls the car at all times.
- Level 1: There is some automation. The car's systems can control steering and speed, but not at the same time.
- Level 2: The car's systems can control steering and speed simultaneously, but the driver remains in control at all times.

- Level 3: The car can drive itself under limited situations. The human driver must remain alert and ready to assume control when needed.
- Level 4: The car can drive itself under most situations. The human driver takes over control in certain situations.
- Level 5: The car can drive itself under all situations and at all times. It has no need for oversight by humans and does not have any manual controls.

Facts and Statistics About Self-Driving Cars

- Self-driving cars may also be called autonomous cars, driverless cars, or robotic cars.
- Seventy-three percent of US drivers think that they have better-than-average driving skills.
- Ninety percent of vehicle crashes occur because of human error, according to the NHTSA.
- According to AAA, in 2017, 78 percent of drivers were afraid to ride in a driverless car.
- According to AAA, in 2018, 63% of drivers were afraid to ride in a driverless car.
- Most of the big automotive companies expect cars with some self-driving capabilities to be on the road by the early 2020s.
- By 2035 to 2040, some predict that 25% of the worldwide car market will be self-driving.
- By 2050, some predict that almost 100% of the worldwide car market will be self-driving.

Organizations to Contact

The editors have compiled the following list of organizations concerned with the issues debated in this book. The descriptions are derived from materials provided by the organizations. All have publications or information available for interested readers. The list was compiled on the date of publication of the present volume; the information provided here may change. Be aware that many organizations take several weeks or longer to respond to inquiries, so allow as much time as possible for the receipt of requested materials.

Carnegie Mellon University (CMU)
5000 Forbes Ave.
Pittsburgh, PA 15213
(412) 268-2000
email: links on site
website: https://www.cmu.edu
CMU is a private university that focuses on global research. At CMU, cutting-edge science happens all the time and ranges from driverless cars and robots to brain science and big data. According to the university, CMU is creating the future.

Department of Transportation and the National Highway Traffic Safety Administration (NHTSA)
1200 New Jersey Ave. SE
Washington, DC 20590
(888) 327-4236
website: https://www.nhtsa.gov
The NHTSA is a governmental agency working to aid the development of driverless car technology. The agency believes this technology has the potential to save lives. The NHTSA actively supports research, education, and enforcement of safety standards to reduce injuries and save lives.

Institute for Transportation and Development Policy
9 E. Nineteenth St., 7th Floor
New York, NY 10003
(212) 629-8001
email: mobility@itdp.org
website: https://www.itdp.org
The Institute for Transportation and Development Policy is a global nonprofit organization that works to build high-quality transportation systems. This agency produces downloadable materials, including a recently published report, *Three Revolutions in Urban Transportation*, which highlights the value of automation and ride sharing for the future of transportation.

Massachusetts Institute of Technology (MIT)
77 Massachusetts Ave.
Cambridge, MA 02139-4307
(617) 253-1000
website: http://www-mtl.mit.edu/researchgroups/itrc/itrc.html
MIT is a university that is committed to educating students ready to take on challenges in areas of benefit to society. One of its research specialties is the Intelligent Transportation Research Center, which looks to solve problems related to future technologies of transportation, including vision systems for intelligent and automated vehicles.

Nuro
435 N. Whisman Rd. #100
Mountain View, CA 94043
email: info@nuro.ai
website: https://nuro.ai
Nuro was founded in 2016 by two engineers dedicated to robotic technology and its potential to benefit everyone. The Nuro team aims to deliver a self-driving vehicle for local goods transportation.

nuTonomy
1 Broadway
Cambridge, MA 02142
(617) 852-2360
email: info@nutonomy.com
website: http://www.nutonomy.com
nuTonomy is a company that builds software for self-driving cars and autonomous robots. It is a spin-off company from MIT and is committed to creating personal mobility for the twenty-first century.

UBER Advanced Technology Group (ATG)
100 32nd St.
Pittsburgh, PA 15201
(412) 587-2986
email: info-atg@uber.com
website: https://www.uber.com/info/atg
The people at UBER's ATG are dedicated to transforming the way of transportation for the world. The engineers at ATG are implementing technologies for self-driving cars and trucks, mapping, and vehicle safety.

Waymo
website: https://www.waymo.com
Waymo is a technology company with a mission to make self-driving transportation an easy and safe way for everyone to get around. In 2009, Waymo began as the self-driving car project at Google, and by 2016, it spun off as an independent organization.

For Further Reading

Books

Berlatsky, Noah. *Artificial Intelligence.* Detroit, MI: Greenhaven Press, 2011.

Analyzes the topic of artificial intelligence from a variety of angles and perspectives. Includes articles by opponents and proponents of the technology, including the opposing effects of transportation safety by AI smart cars.

Carr, Nicholas G. *The Glass Cage: Automation and Us.* New York, NY: W. W. Norton & Company, 2014.

Investigates the issues and headlines of automation and the digital age. Analyzes how software in the form of driverless cars, factory robots, wearable computers and more appears more and more in our lives and may not be the best.

Currie, Stephen. *Self-Driving Car.* Chicago, IL: Norwood House Press, 2017.

Outlines the development and invention of self-driving cars. Explores the challenges and difficulties encountered with this invention and the advances of today.

Fallon, Michael. *Self-Driving Cars: The New Way Forward.* Minneapolis, MN: Twenty-First Century Books, 2018.

Analyzes the next big shift in transportation, the driverless car. Learn how the hardware and software of autonomous cars developed and the challenges of the engineering along the way.

Ferris, Timothy. *The Big Idea: How Breakthroughs of the Past Shape the Future.* New York, NY: National Geographic, 2011.

Presents the world's biggest ideas, breakthroughs, and discoveries and the brilliant personalities behind the accomplishments. Shows where science is pushing into the future.

Lipson, Hod, and Melba Kurman. *Driverless: Intelligent Cars and the Road Ahead.* Cambridge, MA: MIT Press, 2016.

Answers important questions about how the ordinary car of which we are familiar is morphing into the ultimate mobility device. Looks at how it will change lives, businesses, and cities.

Swanson, Jennifer. *Amazing Feats of Electrical Engineering.* Edina, MN: Abdo Publishing, 2015.

Explains in detail examples of engineering feats, ranging from architectural to aeronautic to medical to technological.

Watson, Stephanie. *What Is the Future of Self-Driving Cars?* San Diego, CA: ReferencePoint Press, 2017.

Maintains that much of the technology to make self-driving cars a reality is already available. It reports that people may soon be turning control over to their cars.

Webb, Amy. *The Signals Are Talking: Why Today's Fringe Is Tomorrow's Mainstream.* New York, NY: PublicAffairs, 2016.

Futurist Amy Webb explores the futuristic ideas bubbling up all around society. She looks at artificial intelligence, machine learning, self-driving cars, and other topics and attempts to answer the important questions of how these innovations will change people and society and how to prepare for the changes.

Periodicals and Internet Sources

Barone, Jennifer. "Hands-Free Ride," Scholastic, September 4, 2017. https://scienceworld.scholastic.com/issues/2017-18/090417/hands-free-ride.html.

Boudette, Neal E. "G.M. Says Its Driverless Car Could Be in Fleets by Next Year," *New York Times*, January 12, 2018. https://www.nytimes.com/2018/01/12/business/gm-driverless-car.html.

Brant, Tom. "Who Should Your Self-Driving Car Save in a Crash? You or Pedestrians?," *PC*, June 23, 2016. https://www.pcmag.com/news/345564/who-should-your-self-driving-car-save-in-a-crash-you-or-ped.

Derousseau, Ryan. "What Self-Driving Cars Will Mean for Automakers' Stocks," *Fortune*, September 6, 2016. http://fortune.com/2016/09/06/auto-stocks-tesla-gm-ford/.

Donath, Judith. "Driverless Cars Could Make Transportation Free for Everyone—with a Catch," *Atlantic*, December 22, 2017. https://

www.theatlantic.com/technology/archive/2017/12/self-driving
-cars-free-future/548945/.

Eadicicco, Lisa. "Uber Drivers Aren't Worried About Self-Driving
Cars—Yet," *Time*, April 10, 2017. http://time.com/4729931/uber
-self-driving-cars-2017/.

Gelbart, Jeremy. "You May Not Live Long Enough to Ride a Driverless
Car," *Newsweek*, April 1, 2017. http://www.newsweek.com/you
-may-not-live-long-enough-ride-driverless-car-575305.

Hawkins, Andrew J. "Americans Still Deeply Skeptical About Driverless
Cars: Poll," Verge, January 12, 2018. https://www.theverge.com
/2018/1/12/16883510/self-driving-car-poll-congress-bill-safety.

Kang, Cecilia. "Self-Driving Cars Gain Powerful Ally: The Government," *New York Times*, September 19, 2016. https://www.nytimes
.com/2016/09/20/technology/self-driving-cars-guidelines.html.

Kang, Cecilia. "Where Self-Driving Cars Go to Learn," *New York Times*,
November 11, 2017. https://www.nytimes.com/2017/11/11
/technology/arizona-tech-industry-favorite-self-driving-hub.html.

Knight, Will. "What to Know Before You Get in a Self-Driving Car,"
MIT Technology Review, October 18, 2016. https://www
.technologyreview.com/s/602492/what-to-know-before-you
-get-in-a-self-driving-car/.

Mervis, Jeffrey. "Are We Going Too Fast on Driverless Cars?," Science,
December 14, 2017. http://www.sciencemag.org/news/2017/12/are
-we-going-too-fast-driverless-cars.

Monticello, Mike. "The State of the Self-Driving Car," *Consumer Reports*, March 31, 2016. https://www.consumerreports.org/self
-driving-cars/state-of-the-self-driving-car/.

Morra, James. "How Automakers Handle Handoffs to Self-Driving
Cars," Electronic Design, August 1, 2017. http://www
.electronicdesign.com/automotive/how-automakers-handle
-handoffs-self-driving-cars.

Morris, David Z. "Mercedes-Benz's Self-Driving Cars Would Choose
Passenger Lives over Bystanders," *Fortune*, October 15, 2016. http://
fortune.com/2016/10/15/mercedes-self-driving-car-ethics/.

Naughton, Keith. "Can Detroit Beat Google to the Self-Driving
Car?," *Bloomberg Businessweek*, October 29, 2015. https://

www.bloomberg.com/features/2015-gm-super-cruise
-driverless-car/.

Naughton, Nora. "GM Works to Fulfill Bold Tech Promises," *Detroit News*, December 13, 2017. http://www.detroitnews.com/story /business/autos/mobility/2017/12/13/self-driving-competitors -challenge-gm/108556388/.

Ohnsman, Alan. "On the Road to Self-Driving Cars, Toyota's First Stop Is Crash-Free Camry's," *Forbes*, March 7, 2017. https://www .forbes.com/sites/alanohnsman/2017/03/07/in-the-race-to -perfect-self-driving-cars-toyotas-first-stop-is-crash-free -camrys/#792ee576871d.

Raymundo, Oscar. "Google Explains Why Its Self-Driving Car Crashed into That Bus," *Macworld*, March 11, 2016. https://www.macworld .com/article/3043593/hardware/google-explains-why-its-self -driving-car-crashed-into-that-bus.html.

Shankleman, Jess. "Self-Driving Cars Will Kill Things You Love (and a Few You Hate," Bloomberg, February 13, 2018. https://www .bloomberg.com/news/articles/2018-02-13/self-driving-cars-will -kill-things-you-love-and-a-few-you-hate.

Shepardson, David. "U.S. House Unanimously Approves Sweeping Self-Driving Car Measure," Reuters, September 6, 2017. https:// www.reuters.com/article/us-autos-selfdriving/u-s-house -unanimously-approves-sweeping-self-driving-car-measure -idUSKCN1BH2B2.

Steinmetz, Katy. "Startups Are Laser-Focused on Helping Self-Driving Cars See," *Time*, August 24, 2017. http://time.com/4913686 /startups-laser-focused-helping-self-driving-cars-see/.

Washington Post Editorial Board. "Driving into the Future," *Washington Post*, May 16, 2015. https://www.washingtonpost.com/opinions /the-future-coming-to-a-highway-near-you/2015/05/16 /ee2d2ef0-fa84-11e4-a13c193b1241d51a_story.html?utm _term=.4b741f05a547.

Woodyard, Chris. "AAA: Drivers Becoming Less Fearful of Self-Driving Car Technology," *USA Today*, January 24, 2018. https://www .usatoday.com/story/money/cars/2018/01/24/aaa-drivers -becoming-less-fearful-self-driving-car-tech/1059861001/.

Websites

**HowStuffWorks (https://auto.howstuffworks.com/under-the
-hood/trends-innovations/driverless-car.htm)**
Learn all about the technology that allows cars to be operated with
minimal input from a human driver. Find out about the driverless car
designs thought to be ready in the next decade or so.

LiveScience Tech (https://www.livescience.com/technology)
Learn about all sorts of technology topics, including driverless cars.
Find out about other technology that is used in self-driving cars, such
as artificial intelligence.

Science Friday (https://www.sciencefriday.com)
Learn all about a variety of science and technology. Read and listen to
the latest technology issues surrounding self-driving vehicles.

Index

Picture Credits

Cover Alexander Koerner/Getty Images; p. 10 Robyn Beck/AFP/ Getty Images; p. 14 Shannon Fagan/Photodisc/Getty Images; p. 18 Katarzyna Bialasiewicz/iStock/Thinkstock; p. 24 Stokkete/ Shutterstock.com; p. 28 mevans/Vetta/Getty Images; p. 36 Hero Images/Getty Images; p. 40 Glowimages/Getty Images; p. 43 Jon Berkeley/Ikon Images/Getty Images; p. 48 Arena Creative/ Shutterstock.com; p. 52 Brooks Kraft/Corbis News/Getty Images; p. 56 Natalia Bratslavsky/Shutterstock.com; p. 63 Sjo/iStock Unreleased/Getty Images; p. 68 chombosan/Shutterstock.com; p. 73 Evan El-Amin/Shutterstock.com; p. 75 Robert Cravens/Shutterstock .com; p. 82 Stockbyte/Thinkstock; p. 90 AFP/Getty Images; p. 97 Bloomberg/Getty Images.